Primary Source Readings in
World Religions

D1051485

Primary Source Readings in
World Religions

Jeffrey Brodd

saint mary's press

The publishing team included Steven C. McGlaun, development editor; Lorraine Kilmartin, reviewer; prepress and manufacturing coordinated by the production departments of Saint Mary's Press.

Shutterstock, cover image

Printed in the United States of America

1353

ISBN 978-0-88489-847-4

Library of Congress Cataloging-in-Publication Data

Brodd, Jeffrey.
     Primary source readings in world religions / Jeffrey Brodd.
     p. cm.
ISBN 978-0-88489-847-4 (pbk)
     1. Religions. 2. Sacred books. I. Title.
BL80.3.B755 2009
200—dc22

                                        2008040067

Contents

Jeffrey Brodd is professor of humanities and religious studies at California State University at Sacramento. He received his doctorate in religious studies from the University of California, Santa Barbara, where he studied with such leaders in the field as Ninian Smart and Birger Pearson. He has taught at the College of Wooster, in Ohio, as well as at Winona State University and Saint Mary's University, both in Winona, Minnesota.

Introduction

To learn about the world's religions is to learn about the world. Religion exerts a profound and pervasive influence on the thoughts and actions of individuals and of entire societies. To learn about the world's religions, however, is a difficult challenge. There are a great many religions, and each is made up of a diversity of elements.

To better study religions, scholar Ninian Smart proposes that we approach this diversity by categorizing them into seven dimensions: mythical, doctrinal, experiential, ethical, ritual, social, and material. A variety of methods can be used to study religions—field trips to places of worship, interviews of participants, historical analyses of sacred art or music, and so forth. Learning about the world's religions by means of *Primary Source Readings in World Religions* calls upon the most obvious method of all: to read texts. Reading the right variety of material can go a surprisingly long way toward covering all seven dimensions of religion.

The writings in this book have been selected to represent the seven dimensions. In this book doctrine is featured from the outset, with presentation of Catholic teachings on the study of world religions. You will also encounter creation myths from Africa and Japan, and an Australian Aborigine myth that accounts for the origin of butterflies—while also explaining what happens after death. The highly personal accounts of Saint Augustine and of the great Muslim scholar al-Ghāzāli offer insights into the experiences of conversion and mysticism. There is no clearer example of the ethical dimension than the Ten Commandments, included here in their original biblical form. The text even represents the dimensions we would least likely associate with the written word—the ritual, social, and material dimensions. Readers will "observe" the Lakota Ghost Dance, and they will join a Jewish family as it participates in the rituals of the Passover meal. All three primary Confucian sources reflect the social emphasis of almost everything in the tradition. The material dimension—typically the featured category for field trips and slide shows—is prevalent in the texts too, as the reader visits sacred cities and sites such as the sacred city of Ile Ife in the Yoruba myth and the Kumbum monastery as described by the Dalai Lama.

Another criterion for selecting the writings in this book was to introduce you to highly significant elements of a given religion. Though most chapters feature at least one example of a sacred text, the various other writings run the gamut, from ancient mythological accounts to influential works of philosophers to contemporary literary fiction to personal insights on what it is to live the religious life. In other words the writings represent a wide variety of genres—but they are all relevant for understanding the world's religions. Reading an account of wearing the *hijab,* a type of head covering, as she commutes to work in New York City, for example, is of no less value than is reading from the *Concluding Unscientific Postscripts to Philosophical Fragments,* the most important book of Søren Kierkegaard, possibly the most influential figure in Protestant Christian thought since Martin Luther.

Chapter 1 of this book offers insight into the Catholic perspective on the study of world religions. The book's twelfth and final chapter, "A World of Perspectives," presents a sampling of ideas and practices of religious traditions that happen not to be included elsewhere. Chapters 2–11 feature traditions commonly covered in courses on world religions. After exploring primal religious traditions in chapter 2, the book proceeds, based loosely on geographical and historical sequencing. Chapters 3–5 address Hinduism, Buddhism, and Sikhism, all having originated in South Asia (that is, India and neighboring regions). Chapters 6–8 cover the East Asian traditions of Confucianism, Taoism, and Shinto. Chapters 9–11 feature religions that originated in western Asia: Judaism, Christianity, and Islam.

For all our intentions to present you with appropriately relevant and diverse reading material, we readily admit that eleven chapters with just three primary sources each (and only two in chapter 1) cannot fully represent the rich tapestry of traditions around the globe. But the book offers sound building blocks for expanding your knowledge of the world's religions—and therefore of our world.

Chapter 1

The Catholic Church and World Religions

With more than one billion members worldwide, the Roman Catholic Church plays an enormous role in shaping global events and nurturing the relationships among peoples and nations. In relation to other world religions, the Catholic Church actively promotes understanding, both on the part of its members and among the various religions themselves.

Official Church doctrine encourages Roman Catholics to learn about the beliefs and practices of the world's religious traditions. This has been especially true in the wake of the Second Vatican Council, commonly called Vatican Council II, which occurred from 1962 to 1965. Pope John XXIII convened this worldwide council of Catholic bishops.

One of the Vatican Council II documents addressing the Catholic Church and world religions is the *Declaration on the Relation of the Church to Non-Christian Religions*, also known as *Nostra Aetate*. Pope Paul VI, whose papacy began in June 1963, proclaimed it on October 28, 1965. *Nostra Aetate* emphasizes the common features of the world's religious traditions and specially mentions Hinduism, Buddhism, Islam, and Judaism. It describes Islam and Judaism extensively and in terms that make clear the Catholic perspective of close religious kinship to Muslims (here "Moslems") and Jews. Naturally, the proclamation maintains that Christ, in the words of John 14:6, is "the way, and the truth, and the life" (NRSV). But *Nostra Aetate* also emphasizes that "the Catholic Church rejects nothing that is true and holy" in the various world religions. The proclamation fosters the pursuit of greater understanding of the religions of others.

The second reading in this chapter is an address by Pope Benedict XVI from a "Meeting with Representatives of Other Religions." The address was delivered at the Pope John Paul II Cultural Center in Washington, D.C., on April 17, 2008. The Pope chose a highly appropriate setting for this address. The Cultural Center, according to its mission statement and as noted in the address, seeks to promote the "human search for meaning and purpose in life" in this multicultural world. Washington, D.C., as the nation's capital and as a symbol of the nation's foundational tenets, created the ideal backdrop for the Pope's pleas for religious freedom. Note also Pope Benedict XVI's support for two other pursuits: faith-based education and interreligious dialogue.

The address by Pope Benedict XVI can perhaps best be summarized as a celebration of pluralism and, like the Vatican Council II proclamation *Nostra Aetate,* as a call for greater understanding through appreciation of our common human concerns and quests. Both documents stress that one way we can gain this appreciation is through dialogue with one another.

Declaration on the Relation of the Church to Non-Christian Religions (Nostra Aetate)

by Pope Paul VI

1. In our time, when day by day mankind is being drawn closer together, and the ties between different peoples are becoming stronger, the Church examines more closely the relationship to non-Christian religions. In her task of promoting unity and love among men, indeed among nations, she considers above all in this declaration what men have in common and what draws them to fellowship.

One is the community of all peoples, one their origin, for God made the whole human race to live over the face of the earth. One also is their final goal, God. His providence, His manifestations of goodness, His saving design extend to all men, until that time when the elect will be united in the Holy City, the city ablaze with the glory of God, where the nations will walk in His light.

Men expect from the various religions answers to the unsolved riddles of the human condition, which today, even as in former times, deeply stir the hearts of men: What is man? What is the meaning, the aim of our life? What is moral good, what sin? Whence suffering and what purpose does it serve? Which is the road to true happiness? What are death, judgment and retribution after death? What, finally, is that ultimate inexpressible mystery which encompasses our existence: whence do we come, and where are we going?

2. From ancient times down to the present, there is found among various peoples a certain perception of that hidden power which hovers over the course of things and over the events of human history; at times some indeed have come to the recognition of a Supreme Being, or even of a Father. This perception and recognition penetrates their lives with a profound religious sense.

Religions, however, that are bound up with an advanced culture have struggled to answer the same questions by means of more refined concepts and a more developed language. Thus in Hinduism, men contemplate the divine mystery and express it through an inexhaustible abundance of myths and through searching philosophical inquiry. They seek freedom from the anguish of our human condition either through **ascetical practices** or profound meditation or a flight to God with love and trust. Again, Buddhism, in its various forms, realizes the radical insufficiency of this changeable world; it teaches a way by which men, in a devout and confident spirit, may be able either to acquire the state of perfect liberation, or attain, by their own efforts or through higher help, supreme illumination. Likewise, other religions found everywhere try to counter the restlessness of the human heart, each in its own manner, by proposing "ways," comprising teachings, rules of life, and sacred rites. The Catholic Church rejects nothing that is true and holy in these religions. She regards with sincere reverence those ways of conduct and of life, those precepts and teachings which, though differing in many aspects from the ones

ascetical practices
self-denial of physical pleasures and worldly attachments for the sake of spiritual growth

she holds and sets forth, nonetheless often reflect a ray of that Truth which enlightens all men. Indeed, she proclaims, and ever must proclaim Christ "the way, the truth, and the life" (John 14:6), in whom men may find the fullness of religious life, in whom God has reconciled all things to Himself.

The Church, therefore, exhorts her sons, that through dialogue and collaboration with the followers of other religions, carried out with prudence and love and in witness to the Christian faith and life, they recognize, preserve and promote the good things, spiritual and moral, as well as the socio-cultural values found among these men.

3. The Church regards with esteem also the Moslems. They adore the one God, living and subsisting in Himself; merciful and all-powerful, the Creator of heaven and earth, who has spoken to men; they take pains to submit wholeheartedly to even His inscrutable decrees, just as Abraham, with whom the faith of Islam takes pleasure in linking itself, submitted to God. Though they do not acknowledge Jesus as God, they revere Him as a prophet. They also honor Mary, His virgin Mother; at times they even call on her with devotion. In addition, they await the day of judgment when God will render their deserts to all those who have been raised up from the dead. Finally, they value the moral life and worship God especially through prayer, almsgiving and fasting.

synod
a gathering of Church authorities for the discussion of issues relating to faith and morals

Since in the course of centuries not a few quarrels and hostilities have arisen between Christians and Moslems, this sacred **synod** urges all to forget the past and to work sincerely for mutual understanding and to preserve as well as to promote together for the benefit of all mankind social justice and moral welfare, as well as peace and freedom.

4. As the sacred synod searches into the mystery of the Church, it remembers the bond that spiritually ties the people of the New Covenant to Abraham's stock.

Thus the Church of Christ acknowledges that, according to God's saving design, the beginnings of her faith and her election are found already among the Patriarchs, Moses and the prophets. She professes that all who believe in Christ—Abraham's sons according to faith—are included in the same Patriarch's call, and likewise that the salvation of the Church is mysteriously foreshadowed by the **chosen people's exodus from the land of bondage.** The Church, therefore, cannot forget that she received the revelation of the Old Testament through the people with whom God in His inexpressible mercy concluded the Ancient Covenant. Nor can she forget that she draws sustenance from **the root of that well-cultivated olive tree onto which have been grafted the wild shoots, the Gentiles.**

chosen people's exodus from the land of bondage
reference to the liberation of the Israelites, under the leadership of Moses, from slavery in Egypt

the root of that well-cultivated olive tree onto which have been grafted the wild shoots, the Gentiles
In Romans, chapters 9–11, Paul explains God's plan for the salvation of the Jews; see Romans 12:11–24 for specific references to the "root" and the "olive tree."

Indeed, the Church believes that by His cross Christ, Our Peace, reconciled Jews and Gentiles, making both one in Himself.

The Church keeps ever in mind the words of the Apostle about his kinsmen: "theirs is the sonship and the glory and the covenants and the law and the worship and the promises; theirs are the fathers and from them is the Christ according to the flesh" (Rom. 9:4–5), the Son of the Virgin Mary. She also recalls that the Apostles, the Church's main-stay and pillars, as well as most of the early disciples who proclaimed Christ's Gospel to the world, sprang from the Jewish people.

As Holy Scripture testifies, Jerusalem did not recognize the time of her visitation, nor did the Jews in large number, accept the Gospel; indeed not a few opposed its spreading. Nevertheless, God holds the Jews most dear for the sake of their Fathers; He does not repent of the gifts He makes or of the calls He issues—such is the witness of the Apostle. In company with the Prophets and the same Apostle, the Church awaits that day, known to God alone, on which all peoples will address the Lord in a single voice and "serve him shoulder to shoulder" (Soph. 3:9).

Since the spiritual patrimony common to Christians and Jews is thus so great, this sacred synod wants to foster and recommend that mutual understanding and respect which is the fruit, above all, of biblical and theological studies as well as of fraternal dialogues.

True, the Jewish authorities and those who followed their lead pressed for the death of Christ; still, what happened in **His passion** cannot be charged against all the Jews, without distinction, then alive, nor against the Jews of today. Although the Church is the new people of God, the Jews should not be presented as rejected or accursed by God, as if this followed from the Holy Scriptures. All should see to it, then, that in catechetical work or in the preaching of the word of God they do not teach anything that does not conform to **the truth of the Gospel** and the spirit of Christ.

Furthermore, in her rejection of every persecution against any man, the Church, mindful of the patrimony she shares with the Jews and moved not by political reasons but by the Gospel's spiritual love, decries hatred, persecutions, displays of anti-Semitism, directed against Jews at any time and by anyone.

Besides, as the Church has always held and holds now, Christ underwent His passion and death freely, because of the sins of men and out of infinite love, in order that all may reach salvation. It is, therefore, the burden of the Church's preaching to proclaim the cross of Christ as the sign of God's all-embracing love and as the fountain from which every grace flows.

5. We cannot truly call on God, the Father of all, if we refuse to treat in a brotherly way any man, created as he is in the image of God. Man's relation to God the Father and his relation to men his brothers are so linked together that Scripture says: "He who does not love does not know God" (1 John 4:8).

> **His passion**
> the last hours of Jesus's earthly ministry, during which he underwent the suffering of his trial and Crucifixion at the hands of Roman authorities

> **the truth of the Gospel**
> the "Good News" (from Old English, godspel) of Jesus Christ's saving power

No foundation therefore remains for any theory or practice that leads to discrimination between man and man or people and people, so far as their human dignity and the rights flowing from it are concerned.

The Church reproves, as foreign to the mind of Christ, any discrimination against men or harassment of them because of their race, color, condition of life, or religion. On the contrary, following in the footsteps of the holy Apostles Peter and Paul, this sacred synod ardently implores the Christian faithful to "maintain good fellowship among the nations" (1 Peter 2:12), and, if possible, to live for their part in peace with all men, so that they may truly be sons of the Father who is in heaven.

"Meeting with Representatives of Other Religions: Address of His Holiness Benedict XVI"

My dear friends,

I am pleased to have this occasion to meet with you today. I thank **Bishop Sklba** for his words of welcome, and I cordially greet all those in attendance representing various religions in the United States of America. Several of you kindly accepted the invitation to compose the reflections contained in today's program. For your thoughtful words on how each of your traditions bears witness to peace, I am particularly grateful. Thank you all.

This country has a long history of cooperation between different religions in many spheres of public life. Interreligious prayer services during the national feast of Thanksgiving, joint initiatives in charitable activities, a shared voice on important public issues: these are some ways in which members of different religions come together to enhance mutual understanding and promote the

Bishop Sklba
(Richard J. Sklba) Milwaukee Auxiliary Bishop and chairman of the U.S. bishop's Committee on Ecumenical and Interreligious Affairs; introduced Pope Benedict XVI to the interreligious leaders attending the Cultural Center on April 17, 2008

common good. I encourage all religious groups in America to persevere in their collaboration and thus enrich public life with the spiritual values that motivate your action in the world.

The place where we are now gathered was founded specifically for promoting this type of collaboration. Indeed, the Pope John Paul II Cultural Center seeks to offer a Christian voice to the "human search for meaning and purpose in life" in a world of "varied religious, ethnic and cultural communities" *(Mission Statement)*. This institution reminds us of this nation's conviction that all people should be free to pursue happiness in a way consonant with their nature as creatures endowed with reason and free will.

Americans have always valued the ability to worship freely and in accordance with their conscience. **Alexis de Tocqueville,** the French historian and observer of American affairs, was fascinated with this aspect of the nation. He

Alexis de Tocqueville (1805–1859) French historian who came to the United States in 1831 and 1832; authored the two-volume *Democracy in America*

remarked that this is a country in which religion and freedom are "intimately linked" in contributing to a stable democracy that fosters social virtues and participation in the communal life of all its citizens. In urban areas, it is common for individuals from different cultural backgrounds and religions to engage with one another daily in commercial, social and educational settings. Today, in classrooms throughout the country, young Christians, Jews, Muslims, Hindus, Buddhists, and indeed children of all religions sit side-by-side, learning with one another and from one another. This diversity gives rise to new challenges that spark a deeper reflection on the core principles of a democratic society. May others take heart from your experience, realizing that a united society can indeed arise from a plurality of peoples—**"E pluribus unum"**: "out of many, one"— provided that all recognize religious liberty as a basic civil right (cf. ***Dignitatis Humanae,*** 2).

E pluribus unum Latin, "out of many, one"; motto on the Great Seal of the United States

Dignitatis Humanae document of the Second Vatican Council published by Pope Paul VI in 1965, also known as *Declaration on Religious Freedom*

The task of upholding religious freedom is never completed. New situations and challenges invite citizens and leaders to reflect on how their decisions respect this basic human right. Protecting religious freedom within the rule of law does not guarantee that peoples—particularly minorities—will be spared from unjust forms of discrimination and prejudice. This requires constant effort on the part of all members of society to ensure that citizens are afforded the opportunity to worship peaceably and to pass on their religious heritage to their children.

The transmission of religious traditions to succeeding generations not only helps to preserve a heritage; it also sustains and nourishes the surrounding culture in the present day. The same holds true for dialogue between religions; both the participants and society are enriched. As we grow in understanding of one another, we see that we share an esteem for ethical values, discernable to human reason, which are revered by all peoples of goodwill. The world begs for a common witness to these values. I therefore invite all religious people to view dialogue not only as a means of enhancing mutual understanding, but also as a way of serving society at large. By bearing witness to those moral truths which they hold in common with all men and women of goodwill, religious groups will exert a positive influence on the wider culture, and inspire neighbors, co-workers and fellow citizens to join in the task of strengthening the ties of solidarity. In the words of President Franklin Delano Roosevelt: "no greater thing could come to our land today than a revival of the spirit of faith".

A concrete example of the contribution religious communities make to civil society is faith-based schools. These institutions enrich children both intellectually and spiritually. Led by their teachers to discover the divinely bestowed dignity of each human being, young people learn to respect the beliefs and practices of others, thus enhancing a nation's civic life.

What an enormous responsibility religious leaders have: to imbue society with a profound awe and respect for human life and freedom; to ensure that human dignity is recognized and cherished; to facilitate peace and justice; to teach children what is right, good and reasonable!

There is a further point I wish to touch upon here. I have noticed a growing interest among governments to sponsor programs intended to promote interreligious and intercultural dialogue. These are praiseworthy initiatives. At the same time, religious freedom, interreligious dialogue and faith-based education aim at something more than a consensus regarding ways to implement practical strategies for advancing peace. The broader purpose of dialogue is to discover the truth. What is the origin and destiny of mankind? What are good and evil? What awaits us at the end of our earthly existence? Only by addressing these deeper questions can we build a solid basis for the peace and security of the human family, for "wherever and whenever men and women are enlightened by the splendor of truth, they naturally set out on the path of peace" (*Message for the 2006 World Day of Peace, 3*).

We are living in an age when these questions are too often marginalized. Yet they can never be erased from the human heart. Throughout history, men and women have striven to articulate their restlessness with this passing world. In the Judeo-Christian tradition, the Psalms are full of such expressions: "My spirit is overwhelmed within me" (Ps 143:4; cf. Ps 6:6; 31:10; 32:3; 38:8; 77:3); "why are you cast down, my soul, why groan within me?" (Ps 42:5). The response is always one of faith: "Hope in God, I will praise him still; my Savior and my God" (Ps 42:5, 11; cf. Ps 43:5; 62:5). Spiritual leaders have a special duty, and we might say competence, to place the deeper questions at the forefront of human consciousness, to reawaken mankind to the mystery of human existence, and to make space in a frenetic world for reflection and prayer.

Confronted with these deeper questions concerning the origin and destiny of mankind, Christianity proposes Jesus of Nazareth. He, we believe, is the eternal Logos who became flesh in order to reconcile man to God and reveal the under-lying reason of all things. It is he whom we bring to the fo-rum of interreligious dialogue. The ardent desire to follow in his footsteps spurs Christians to open their minds and hearts in dialogue (cf. Lk 10:25–37; Jn 4:7–26).

Dear friends, in our attempt to discover points of com-monality, perhaps we have shied away from the responsi-bility to discuss our differences with calmness and clarity. While always uniting our hearts and minds in the call for peace, we must also listen attentively to the voice of truth. In this way, our dialogue will not stop at identifying a common set of values, but go on to probe their ultimate foundation. We have no reason to fear, for the truth unveils for us the essential relationship between the world and God. We are able to perceive that peace is a "heavenly gift" that calls us to conform human history to the divine order. Herein lies the "truth of peace" (cf. *Message for the 2006 World Day of Peace*).

As we have seen then, the higher goal of interreligious dialogue requires a clear exposition of our respective reli-gious tenets. In this regard, colleges, universities and study

Holy See
derived from the Latin *sancta sedes,* meaning "holy chair," it consists of the Pope of the Roman Catholic Church, together with the institutional hierarchy of authorities (that is, the bishops)

centers are important forums for a candid exchange of religious ideas. The **Holy See,** for its part, seeks to carry forward this important work through the Pontifical Council for Interreligious Dialogue, the Pontifical Institute for Arabic and Islamic Studies, and various Pontifical Universities.

Dear friends, let our sincere dialogue and cooperation inspire all people to ponder the deeper questions of their origin and destiny. May the followers of all religions stand together in defending and promoting life and religious freedom everywhere. By giving ourselves generously to this sacred task—through dialogue and countless small acts of love, understanding and compassion—we can be instruments of peace for the whole human family.

Peace upon you all!

For Reflection

1. *Nostra Aetate* identifies several "unsolved riddles of the human condition." What are they? In what ways and to what extent does society today treat such riddles as relevant?

2. Through *Nostra Aetate* the Catholic Church in 1965 condemned "any discrimination against men or harassment of them because of their race, color, condition of life, or religion." Based on your experiences and observations, to what extent does today's society agree with these teachings?

3. According to Pope Benedict XVI, what questions does interreligious dialogue help answer? How are religious freedom and faith-based education related to interreligious dialogue?

4. In your own words, explain the perspective of the Catholic Church on the study of world religions. Quote specific references from both readings in chapter 1 to support your explanation.

Chapter 2

Primal Religious Traditions

The phrase *primal religious traditions* refers to the religious traditions of native peoples, because these traditions have tended to come first, before the arrival of "global" religions such as Christianity and Islam. Primal traditions tend to be confined to relatively small groups of people. In this chapter we consider three primary sources from three distinct traditions. The first two sources are myths, one from Australia and the other from Africa. The third source describes a ritual practice of the Lakota, a people of the North American Great Plains. The emphasis on myth and ritual in this chapter is in keeping with the general trend of primal traditions to emphasize these aspects of religion.

Religion among the Australian Aborigines, the original inhabitants of Australia, is grounded in a belief in a mythic period known as the Dreaming. Aborigines believe that during the Dreaming, prehuman beings established the natural world and, eventually, human society. The myth included here relates the origin of butterflies. This myth answers a fundamental question for the Aboriginal people: What happens to a person after death? Myths often provide explanations to such basic human concerns.

This story exhibits common features of myths. A myth is typically set in an era in the distant past, or primordial time, before the complete establishment of the world as we know it. Note that this story begins "Long ago, before a race of men inhabited Australia . . ." Note also that the story makes early mention of "wise old men" and "medicine-men"—but that these "men" are actually members of the animal kingdom. Supernatural beings, be they gods and goddesses or such natural beings as animals with the powers of speech and reasoning, commonly populate myths.

A myth is always a story, a narrative with a beginning and an end. A myth is not *authored* in our usual sense of the word. Instead of having been written by an individual, a myth somehow has come to be through many generations of oral storytelling. A myth thus sets forth the beliefs of a group of people, not just the particular perspectives of one person. The myth of the origin of the butterflies contains crucial answers to some of life's basic questions. It may be read simply as an entertaining story, but for the Australian Aborigines who have traditionally told it, it is a story that contains profound truths.

The second myth in this chapter is from the Yoruba people of central Africa. The Yoruba believe in the existence of many deities, called *orishas*. Along with the supreme god, Olodumare, one of the most significant *orishas* is the creator god, Obatalá. The Yoruba myth presented here recounts the creation of the world by Obatalá. Note that it shares many of the common features of myth we observe in the Australian story.

The third reading is Mary Crow Dog's description of the Ghost Dance, a ritual popular among the Lakota and other native North American nations during the late nineteenth century. Leonard Crow Dog, a medicine man and leading figure among the Lakota during the 1970s (and eventually the husband of the author), revived the Ghost Dance.

The dance had already led to conflict at Wounded Knee, South Dakota. In 1890 U.S. soldiers killed more than two hundred Native Americans during a Ghost Dance. In 1973 Wounded Knee was again the site of hostilities with federal FBI agents. When reading Mary Crow Dog's account, note that the ritual, both in its traditional and more modern manifestations, was intended to help the people connect to their sacred foundations, most especially to the "sacred hoop" and to their deceased ancestors. Connecting to sacred foundations is a common function of religious ritual.

Australian Aborigines: Excerpt from *Myths and Legends of the Australian Aboriginals*

"The Birth of the Butterflies"

Long ago, before a race of men inhabited Australia, the animals could talk with one another, and they had no experience of death. All through the summer months it was the custom of the different tribes, the animals, the birds, and the reptiles, to gather together on the banks of the **river Murray** in order to enjoy the cool

river Murray
Australia's principal river, rising in the mountains of the southeast and emptying into the Indian Ocean on the west

waters of the river and the shade of the gum-trees. The **wise old men** of the tribes used to sit and talk, while the younger members enjoyed themselves at play and sports.

One day a young cockatoo fell from a high tree and broke his neck. He lay dead on the ground. All the animals gathered round to try to wake him. They touched him with a spear, but he could not feel. They opened his eyes, but he could not see. The animals were completely mystified, for they did not understand death. Then all the medicine-men tried to awaken the cockatoo, but without success.

A general meeting was called to discuss the matter of the dead bird. First of all the owl, who with his great eyes was supposed to be very wise, was called upon to speak. But the owl was silent. Then the eagle-hawk, the great chief of the birds, was asked to explain this mystery of death. The eagle-hawk took a pebble and threw it out into the river, and all the onlookers saw the pebble strike the water and disappear from sight. Turning to the tribes the eagle-hawk cried, "There is the explanation of the mystery; as the pebble has entered on another existence so has the cockatoo."

This explanation, however, did not satisfy the gathering; so they next asked the crow to speak. Although all of them knew that the crow was very wicked, they also knew he had great knowledge. The crow stepped forward and took up a

wit-wit

a thin throwing stick,
a common plaything
among Australian
Aborigines

wit-wit and threw it into the river. The weapon sank, and then gradually rose again to the surface. "There," said the crow, "is the great mystery explained. We all go through another world of experience, and then return."

Now this explanation impressed all the tribes, and the eagle-hawk asked, "Who will volunteer to go through this experience and test it, and see if it is possible to return?" Certain of the animal and reptile tribes offered to make the test. "Very well," said the eagle-hawk, "but you must go through the experience of not being sensible to sight, taste, smell, touch, or hearing, and then return to us in another form."

When it became winter-time all the creatures that creep into holes and hollow logs and sleep during the winter months went away—the goanna, the opossum, the wombat, and the snake.

In the following spring the tribes gathered together again to wait the return of those who were trying to solve the great mystery. At last the goanna, the opossum, the wombat, and the snake returned, all looking half starved. When they showed themselves to the gathering the eagle-hawk said, "You have all returned in the same form as you went out, although the snake has half changed his skin."

Still the gathering was anxious to solve the mystery of death. At last the insect tribe, the moths, the water-bugs, and the caterpillars, volunteered to try to find a solution of that mystery. All the others, and especially the laughing jacks, ridiculed this, because the insects had always been looked upon as ignorant and stupid. The insects persisted, so the eagle-hawk gave them permission to try. But the insects did not crawl away out of sight. The water-bugs asked to be wrapped in a fine bark and thrown into the river. Some asked to be put in the bark of trees; and others to be placed under the ground. "Now," said the different bugs and caterpillars, "we will return at the spring-time of the year in another form, and we will meet you in the mountains." The tribes then dispersed until the following spring.

All the animals knew by the position of the stars at night when spring-time was approaching. As it drew near there was great excitement everywhere. The animals felt that the mystery would now be solved. The day before the time fixed for the return of the insects the eagle-hawk sent out notice, and all the animals, birds, and reptiles gathered in the mountains to await the great event. That night the dragon-flies, the gnats, and the fireflies came round the camp-fires as heralds of the wonderful pageant that was to take place on the morrow. Already the trees, the shrubs, and the flowers had consented to lend themselves for the occasion. The dragonfly went from camp to camp and from tribe to tribe, telling every one what a marvellous sight it was going to be, to see all the insects returning from the dead in their new bodies.

At daybreak every animal, bird, and reptile was out to witness the arrival of the pageant. The **wattle** put forth all its wonderful yellow, and the **waratah** its brilliant red,

wattle
acacia plant

waratah
a flowering shrub

and all the other flowers showed their blossoms of varied colours.

Just as the sun rose over the tops of the hills the dragon-flies came up through the entrance of the mountains heading an array of butterflies. Each species and colour of butterfly came in order. First the yellow came up and showed themselves. They flew about and rested upon the trees and the flowers. Then came the red, the blue, the green, and so right on through all the families.

The animals were delighted. They gave great cries of admiration. The birds were so pleased that, for the first time, they broke forth into song. Everything looked its best. When the last of the butterflies had entered the mountains they asked the great gathering, "Have we solved the mystery of death? Have we returned in another form?" And all nature answered back, "You have."

And all this can be seen at the return of every springtime.

The Yoruba: Excerpt from *The Altar of My Soul: The Living Traditions of Santeria*

Creation Myth

Olodumare
also known as Olorun in
Yoruba mythology

The *orisha* **Olodumare**, the Supreme God, originally lived in the lower part of heaven, overlooking endless stretches of water. One day, Olodumare decided to create Earth, and sent an emissary, the *orisha* **Obatalá,** to perform this task. Olodumare gave Obatalá the

materials he needed to create the world: a small bag of loose earth, a gold chain, and a five-toed hen.

Obatalá was instructed to use the chain to descend from heaven. When he reached the last link, he piled the loose earth on top of the water. Next, he placed the hen on the pile of earth, and ordered her to scatter the earth with her toes across the surface of the water.

When this was finished, Obatalá climbed the chain to heaven to report his success to Olodumare. Olodumare then sent his trusted assistant, the chameleon, to verify that the earth was dry. When his helper had assured him that the Earth was solid, Olodumare named Earth "Ile Ife," the sacred house.

Before he retired to the uppermost level of heaven, Olodumare decided to distribute his sacred powers—*ache.* He united Obatalá, the *orisha* of creation, and Yemayá, the *orisha* of the ocean, who gave birth to a pantheon of *orishas,* each possessing a share of Olodumare's sacred power. At last, the divine power of Olodumare was dispersed. Then one day, Olodumare called them all from Earth to heaven and gave Obatalá the sacred power to create human life. Obatalá returned to Earth and created our ancestors, endowing them with his own divine power. We are all descendants from the first people of the sacred city of Ile Ife; we are all children of Olodumare, the sacred *orisha* who created the world.

The Lakota: Excerpt from *Lakota Woman*

"On the Ghost Dance," by Mary Crow Dog

Leonard [Crow Dog, the author's husband] always thought that the **dancers of 1890** had misunderstood **Wovoka** and his message. They should not have expected to bring the dead back to life, but to bring back their ancient beliefs by practicing Indian religion. For Leonard, dancing in a circle holding hands was bringing back the **sacred hoop** —to feel, holding on to the hand of your brother and sister, the rebirth of Indian unity, feel it with your flesh, through your skin. He also thought that reviving the Ghost Dance would be making a link to our past, to the grandfathers and grandmothers of long ago. So he decided to ghost-dance again at the **place where this dance had been killed** and where now it had to be resurrected. He knew all the songs and rituals that his father Henry had taught him, who himself had learned them from his

> **dancers of 1890**
> The Ghost Dance was a main factor leading to the massacre at Wounded Knee in 1890.

> **Wovoka** (1856?–1932) also known by his Christian name, Jack Wilson, a member of the Paiute community in western Nevada, who, in 1889, experienced a vision on which he based his teachings of the Ghost Dance to Native Americans across the West

grandfather. All through the night women were making old-style Ghost Dance shirts out of curtains, burlap bags, or whatever they could find. They painted them in the traditional way and they were beautiful.

On the evening before the dance, Leonard addressed the people. We got it down on tape. This is what he said: "Tomorrow we'll ghost-dance. You're not goin' to say 'I got to rest.' There'll be no rest, no intermission, no coffee break. We're not going to drink water. So that'll take place whether it snows or rains. We're goin' to unite together, no matter what tribe we are. We won't say, 'I'm a different tribe,' or, 'He's a black man, he's a white man.' We're not goin' to have this white man's attitude.

"If one of us gets into the power, the spiritual power, we'll hold hands. If he falls down, let him. If he goes into convulsions, don't be scared. We won't call a medic. The spirit's goin' to be the doctor.

"There's a song I'll sing, a song from the spirit. Mother Earth is the drum, and the clouds will be the visions. The visions will go into your mind. In your mind you might see your brothers, your relations that have been killed by the white man.

sacred hoop
symbolic of the traditional Lakota way of life, Nicholas Black Elk and others understood the sacred hoop as having been broken due to the massacre at Wounded Knee in 1890; mending the hoop symbolizes the return of health and prosperity to the Lakota people

place where this dance had been killed
reference to Wounded Knee massacre of 1890

"We'll elevate ourselves from this world to another world from where you can see. It's here that we're goin' to find out, The Ghost Dance spirit will be in us. The **peace pipe** is goin' to be there. The fire is goin' to be there; tobacco is goin' to be there. We'll start physically and go on spiritually and then you'll get into the power. We're goin' to start right here, at Wounded Knee, in 1973.

"Everybody's heard about the Ghost Dance but nobody's ever seen it. The United States prohibited it. There was to be no Ghost Dance, no **Sun Dance,** no Indian religion.

"But the hoop has not been broken. So decide tonight— for the whole unborn generations. If you want to dance with me tomorrow, you be ready!"

> **peace pipe**
> a sacred pipe, also called a calumet, ritually smoked; often used to accompany other Native American rituals

> **Sun Dance**
> ritual of the Lakota and many other Native American peoples, performed in late spring or early summer in a specially constructed circular enclosure or lodge

For the dance, Leonard had selected a hollow between hills where the feds could neither see the dancers nor shoot at them. And he had made this place wakan—sacred. And so the Sioux were ghost-dancing again, for the first time in over eighty years. They danced for four days starting at five o'clock in the morning, dancing from darkness into the night. And that dance took place around the first day of spring, a new spring for the Sioux Nation. Like the Ghost Dancers of old, many men danced barefoot in the snow around a cedar tree. Leonard had about thirty or forty dancers. Not everybody who wanted to was able to dance. Nurses and medics had to remain at their stations. Life had to be sustained and the defenses maintained.

On the first day, one of the women fell down in the snow and was helped back to what used to be the museum. They smoked the pipe and Leonard **cedared** her, fanning her with his eagle wing. Slowly she came to. The woman said she could not verbalize what had happened to her, but that she was in the power and had received a vision. It took her a long time to say that much because she was in a trance with only the whites of her eyes showing. On one of the four days a snowstorm interrupted the dancing, but it could not stop it. Later, Wallace Black Elk thanked the dancers for their endurance and Russel Means made a good speech about the significance of the rebirth of the Ghost Dance.

The **Oglala holy man Black Elk,** who died some fifty years ago, in his book said this about Wounded Knee: "I can still see the butchered women and children lying heaped and scattered all along the crooked gulch as plain as when I saw them with eyes still young. And I can see something else died there in the bloody mud, and was buried in the blizzard. A people's dream died there. It was a beautiful dream.

cedared
ritually fanned with the smoke of a burning cedar bough

Oglala holy man Black Elk
The Oglala are the largest of seven bands of the Lakota; Black Elk memorialized the plight of his people in *Black Elk Speaks*, by John Neihardt.

"And I, to whom so great a vision was given in my youth—you see me now a pitiful old man who has done nothing, for the nation's hoop is broken and scattered. There is no center any longer, and the sacred tree is dead."

In that ravine, at **Cankpe Opi,** we gathered up the broken pieces of the sacred hoop and put them together again. All who were at Wounded Knee, Buddy Lamont, Clearwater, and our medicine men, we mended the nation's hoop. The sacred tree is not dead!

Cankpe Opi
Lakota name for
Wounded Knee

For Reflection

1. The Aboriginal myth recounts that various animals try to explain to the tribes what has happened to the dead cockatoo. Why do you think the crow is able to provide the correct explanation?

2. Explain how the arrival of the butterflies verifies the crow's explanation. What does this mythic explanation suggest regarding the Aborigines' beliefs about death and the afterlife?

3. Read Genesis, chapters 1 and 2, and compare them with the Yoruba creation story. What are the most notable similarities and differences?

4. Based on your reading of Mary Crow Dog's account, describe the Ghost Dance as it was practiced at Wounded Knee in 1973.

Chapter 3

Hinduism

Hinduism embraces a diverse set of religious paths, all leading to the same goal: liberation (or *moksha*) from the limitations of the human condition. Most Hindus understand this liberation to coincide with complete union with ultimate reality, called Brahman. Just as they embrace many religious paths within their own broad tradition, Hindus also tend to be highly tolerant of other religions. This chapter's three primary sources illustrate in various ways basic Hindu perspectives.

The Bhagavad-Gita, Hinduism's most popular sacred text, is a short section of one of the world's longest poems, the *Mahabharata*. *The Bhagavad-Gita* was completed in its present form by the second century AD. It presents a dialogue between Arjuna, a great warrior, and Krishna, an incarnation of God who has assumed the role of Arjuna's chariot driver. Krishna counsels Arjuna, who, in the First Teaching (there are seventeen altogether), expressed his anguish over the circumstances that call for him to go to war against relatives and friends. In this chapter's excerpt, the Second and Third Teachings, Krishna responds by explaining fundamental ideas of Hinduism. One idea is that of reincarnation. As Krishna explains, the warriors who die in this fight are destined to be reincarnated and to resume living in another body. From this perspective no one ever really kills or is killed. A second idea is that of sacred duty, or *dharma*. Because Arjuna was born a warrior, it is his sacred duty to fight this war. In the Third Teaching, Krishna emphasizes *Karma marga*, or the path of action. Note how Krishna teaches that Arjuna must act but that in doing so he must remain "detached" from the effects of his actions. The final objective of all Hindu religious paths is liberation from the human limitations and union with Brahman. Note Krishna's various references to this ultimate reality: "indestructible . . . presence," "infinite spirit," and the like.

The second reading deals with Vedanta. This is a prominent Hindu system of philosophy whose most important proponent was the medieval philosopher Shankara (spelled Śaṅkara in the excerpt). A foundational doctrine of Vedanta is monism, a belief in one unchanging and eternal reality known as Brahman. The two elephant anecdotes included here are traditional teaching stories of Vedanta. Both stories address a challenging question: if, as the doctrine of monism holds, all reality is essentially Brahman, unchanging and eternal, why do we human beings perceive reality as consisting of many things that are changeable? Vedanta's answer rests in the doctrine of *maya*, or cosmic illusion. We humans, due to our ignorance, tend to mistake the illusion for reality. When reading the anecdotes, note that *maya* does indeed seem real for those under its spell, much as a dream seems perfectly real while one is still dreaming.

Mohandas Gandhi, sometimes titled *Mahatma*, believed that "Truth is God" and that God is to be found through love. These beliefs underlay his entire philosophy of nonviolence and have left an indelible mark on the nature of Hinduism.

Note how these basic beliefs lead naturally both to Gandhi's insistence that political action must be based on religion and to his outspoken tolerance for other religions. Not coincidentally Gandhi revered *The Bhagavad-Gita* and the Gospel of Matthew's Sermon on the Mount as his favorite sacred texts.

Excerpts from *The Bhagavad-Gita*

The Second and Third Teachings

The Second Teaching: Philosophy and Spiritual Discipline

Sanjaya

Arjuna sat dejected,
filled with pity,
his sad eyes blurred by tears.
Krishna gave him counsel.

Lord Krishna

Why this cowardice
in time of crisis, Arjuna?
The coward is ignoble,
    shameful,
foreign to the ways of heaven.

Don't yield to impotence!
It is unnatural in you!

Banish this petty weakness from
    your heart.

Rise to the fight, Arjuna!

Arjuna

Krishna, how can I fight
against **Bhishma and Drona**

Sanjaya
Adviser to the blind king Dhritarashtra, Sanjaya narrates to the king the events of the epic battle in which the dialogue between Arjuna and Krishna is set.

with arrows
when they deserve my worship?
It is better in this world
to beg for scraps of food
than to eat meals
smeared with the blood
of elders I killed
at the height of their power
while their goals
were still desires.

We don't know which weight
is worse to bear—
our conquering them
or their conquering us.

Bhishma and Drona
two teachers of the martial
arts whom Arjuna reveres
but who fight on the opposite side in this war

sons of Dhritarashtra
one hundred brothers who
fight against their cousin
Arjuna and his brothers

sacred duties
because Arjuna was born
into the Kshatriya, or warrior, class, it is his *dharma*,
or sacred duty, to fight

We will not want to live
if we kill
the **sons of Dhritarashtra**
      assembled before us.

The flaw of pity
blights my very being;
conflicting **sacred duties**
confound my reason.
I ask you to tell me
decisively—Which is better?
I am your pupil.
Teach me what I seek!
I see nothing
that could drive away
the grief
that withers my senses;
even if I won kingdoms
of unrivaled wealth
on earth
and sovereignty over gods.

Sanjaya

Arjuna told this
to Krishna—then saying,
"I shall not fight,"
he fell silent.

Mocking him gently,
Krishna gave this counsel
as Arjuna sat dejected
between the two armies.

Lord Krishna

You grieve for those beyond
    grief,
and you speak words of insight;
but learned men do not grieve
for the dead or the living.

Never have I not existed,
nor you, nor these kings;
and never in the future
shall we cease to exist.

Just as the embodied self
enters childhood, youth, and
    old age,
so does it enter another body;
this does not confound a
    steadfast man.

Contacts with matter make us
    feel
heat and cold, pleasure and
    pain.
Arjuna, you must learn to
    endure
fleeting things—they come and
    go!

When these cannot torment a
    man,
when suffering and joy are
    equal
for him and he has courage,
he is fit for immortality.

Nothing of nonbeing comes to
    be,
nor does being cease to exist;
the boundary between these
    two
is seen by men who see reality.

Indestructible is the presence
that pervades all this;
no one can destroy
this unchanging reality.

Our bodies are known to end,
but the embodied self is
    enduring,
indestructible, and
    immeasurable;
therefore, Arjuna, fight the
    battle!

He who thinks this self a killer
and he who thinks it killed,
    both fail to understand;
it does not kill, nor is it killed.

It is not born,
it does not die;
having been,
it will never not be;
unborn, enduring,
constant, and primordial,
it is not killed
when the body is killed.

Arjuna, when a man knows the
    self
to be indestructible, enduring,
    unborn,

unchanging, how does he kill
or cause anyone to kill?

As a man discards
worn-out clothes
to put on new
and different ones,
so the embodied self
discards
its worn-out bodies
to take on other new ones.

Weapons do not cut it,
fire does not burn it,
waters do not wet it,
wind does not wither it.

It cannot be cut or burned;
it cannot be wet or withered;
it is enduring, all-pervasive,
fixed, immovable, and timeless.

It is called unmanifest,
inconceivable, and immutable;
since you know that to be so,
you should not grieve!

If you think of its birth
and death as ever-recurring,
then too, Great Warrior,
you have no cause to grieve!
Death is certain for anyone
    born,
and birth is certain for the dead;
since the cycle is inevitable,
you have no cause to grieve!

Creatures are unmanifest in
    origin,
manifest in the midst of life,
and unmanifest again in the
    end.
Since this is so, why do you
    lament?

Rarely someone
sees it,
rarely another
speaks it,
rarely anyone hears it—
even hearing it,
no one really knows it.

The self embodied in the body
of every being is indestructible;
you have no cause to grieve
for all these creatures, Arjuna!

Look to your own duty;
do not tremble before it;
nothing is better for a warrior
than a battle of sacred duty.

The doors of heaven open
for warriors who rejoice

to have a battle like this
thrust on them by chance.

If you fail to wage this war
of sacred duty,
you will abandon your own
    duty
and fame only to gain evil.

People will tell
of your undying shame,
and for a man of honor
shame is worse than death.

The great chariot warriors will
    think
you deserted in fear of battle;
you will be despised
by those who held you in
    esteem.

Your enemies will slander you,
scorning your skill
in so many unspeakable ways—
could any suffering be worse?

If you are killed, you win
    heaven;
if you triumph, you enjoy the
    earth;
therefore, Arjuna, stand up
and resolve to fight the battle!

Impartial to joy and suffering,
gain and loss, victory and
    defeat,
arm yourself for the battle,
lest you fall into evil.

Understanding is defined in
    terms of philosophy;
now hear it in spiritual
    discipline.
Armed with this understanding,
    Arjuna,
you will escape the bondage of
    action.

No effort in this world
is lost or wasted;
a fragment of sacred duty
saves you from great fear.

This understanding is unique
in its inner core of resolve;
diffuse and pointless are the
    ways
irresolute men understand.

Undiscerning men who delight
in the tenets of ritual lore
utter florid speech, proclaiming,
"There is nothing else!"

Driven by desire, they strive
    after heaven
and contrive to win powers and
    delights,
but their intricate ritual
    language
bears only the fruit of action in
    rebirth.

Obsessed with powers and
    delights,
their reason lost in words,
they do not find in
    contemplation
this understanding of inner
    resolve.

Arjuna, the realm of sacred lore
is nature—beyond its triad of
    qualities,
dualities, and mundane
    rewards,

be forever lucid, alive to your
self.

For the discerning priest,
all of sacred lore
has no more value than a well
when water flows everywhere.

Be intent on action,
not on the fruits of action;
avoid attraction to the fruits
and attachment to inaction!

Perform actions, firm in
discipline,
relinquishing attachment;
be impartial to failure and
success—
this equanimity is called
discipline.

Arjuna, action is far inferior
to the discipline of
understanding;
so seek refuge in
understanding—pitiful
are men drawn by fruits of
action.

Disciplined by understanding,
one abandons both good and
evil deeds;
so arm yourself for discipline—
discipline is skill in actions.

Wise men disciplined by
understanding

relinquish the fruit born of
action;
freed from these bonds of
rebirth,
they reach a place beyond
decay.

When your understanding
passes beyond
the swamp of delusion,
you will be indifferent to all
that is heard in sacred lore.

When your understanding turns
from sacred lore to stand fixed,
immovable in contemplation,
then you will reach discipline.

Arjuna

Krishna, what defines a man
deep in contemplation whose
insight
and thought are sure? How
would he speak?
How would he sit? How would
he move?

Lord Krishna

When he gives up desires in his
mind,
is content with the self within
himself,
then he is said to be a man
whose insight is sure, Arjuna.

When suffering does not disturb
    his mind,
when his craving for pleasures
    has vanished,
when attraction, fear, and anger
    are gone,
he is called a sage whose
    thought is sure.

When he shows no preference
in fortune or misfortune
and neither exults nor hates,
his insight is sure.

When, like a tortoise retracting
its limbs, he withdraws his
    senses
completely from sensuous
    objects,
his insight is sure.

Sensuous objects fade
when the embodied self ab-
    stains from food;
the taste lingers, but it too fades
in the vision of higher truth.

Even when a man of wisdom
tries to control them, Arjuna,
the bewildering senses
attack his mind with violence.

Controlling them all,
with discipline he should focus
    on me;

when his senses are under
    control,
his insight is sure.

Brooding about sensuous
    objects
makes attachment to them
    grow;
from attachment desire arises,
from desire anger is born.

From anger comes confusion;
from confusion memory lapses;
from broken memory
    understanding is lost;
from loss of understanding, he
    is ruined.

But a man of inner strength
whose senses experience
    objects
without attraction and hatred,
in self-control, finds serenity.

In serenity, all his sorrows
dissolve;
his reason becomes serene,
his understanding sure.

Without discipline,
he has no understanding or
    inner power;
without inner power, he has no
    peace;
and without peace where is
    joy?

If his mind submits to the play
of the senses,
they drive away insight,
as wind drives a ship on water.

So, Great Warrior, when
    withdrawal
of the senses
from sense objects is complete,
discernment is firm.

When it is night for all
    creatures,
a master of restraint is awake;
when they are awake, it is night
for the sage who sees reality.

As the mountainous depths
of the ocean
are unmoved when waters
rush into it,

so the man unmoved
when desires enter him
attains a peace that eludes
the man of many desires.
When he renounces all desires
and acts without craving,
possessiveness,
or individuality, he finds peace.
This is the place of the infinite
    spirit;
achieving it, one is freed from
    delusion;
abiding in it even at the time of
    death,
one finds the pure calm of
    infinity.

The Third Teaching: Discipline of Action

Arjuna

If you think understanding
is more powerful than action,
why, Krishna, do you urge me
to this horrific act?

You confuse my understanding
with a maze of words;
speak one certain truth
so I may achieve what is good.

Lord Krishna

Earlier I taught the twofold
basis of good in this world—
for philosophers, disciplined
    knowledge;
for men of discipline, action.

A man cannot escape the force
of action by abstaining from
    actions;

he does not attain success
just by renunciation.

No one exists for even an
    instant
without performing action;
however unwilling, every being
    is forced
to act by the qualities of nature.

When his senses are controlled
but he keeps recalling
sense objects with his mind,
he is a self-deluded hypocrite.

When he controls his senses
with his mind and engages in
    the discipline
of action with his faculties of
    action,
detachment sets him apart.

Perform necessary action;
it is more powerful than
    inaction;
without action you even fail
to sustain your own body.

Action imprisons the world
unless it is done as sacrifice;
freed from attachment, Arjuna,
perform action as sacrifice!

When creating living beings
    and sacrifice,
Prajapati, the primordial
    creator, said:

"By sacrifice will you
procreate!
Let it be your wish-granting
cow!

Foster the gods with this,
and may they foster you;
by enriching one another,
you will achieve a higher
good.

Enriched by sacrifice, the
gods
will give you the delights
you desire;
he is a thief who enjoys
their gifts
without giving to them in
return."

Good men eating the remnants
of sacrifice are free of any guilt,
but evil men who cook for
    themselves
eat the food of sin.

Creatures depend on food,
food comes from rain,
rain depends on sacrifice,

Prajapati
(Sanskrit, "Lord of
Creatures") a prominent
creator god in early Hindu
literature

and sacrifice comes from action.

Action comes from the spirit of prayer,
whose source is **OM,** sound of the imperishable;
so the pervading infinite spirit
is ever present in rites of sacrifice.

He who fails to keep turning
the wheel here set in motion
wastes his life in sin,
addicted to the senses, Arjuna.

But when a man finds delight
within himself and feels inner joy

OM
a sacred syllable that is pronounced prior to worship
or to the reading of certain
sacred texts

Janaka
legendary king of ancient
India

three worlds
the netherworlds, earth,
and heaven

and pure contentment in him-self,
there is nothing more to be done.

He has no stake here
in deeds done or undone,
nor does his purpose
depend on other creatures.
Always perform with detachment
any action you must do;
performing action with detachment,
one achieves supreme good.

Janaka and other ancient kings
attained perfection by action alone;
seeing the way to preserve
the world, you should act.

Whatever a leader does,
the ordinary people also do.
He sets the standard
for the world to follow.

In the **three worlds,**
there is nothing I must do,
nothing unattained to be attained,
yet I engage in action.

What if I did not engage
relentlessly in action?
Men retrace my path
at every turn, Arjuna.

These worlds would collapse
if I did not perform action;
I would create disorder in
     society,
living beings would be
     destroyed.

As the ignorant act with
     attachment
to actions, Arjuna,
so wise men should act with
     detachment
to preserve the world.

No wise man disturbs the
     understanding
of ignorant men attached to
     action;
he should inspire them,
performing all actions with
     discipline.

Actions are all effected
by the qualities of nature;
but deluded by individuality,
the self thinks, "I am the actor."

When he can discriminate
the actions of nature's qualities
and think, "The qualities
     depend
on other qualities," he is
     detached.

Those deluded by the qualities
     of nature
are attached to their actions;

a man who knows this should
     not upset
these dull men of partial
     knowledge.

Surrender all actions to me,
and fix your reason on your
     inner self;
without hope or possessiveness,
your fever subdued, fight the
     battle!

Men who always follow my
     thought,
trusting it without finding fault,
are freed
even by their actions.

But those who find fault
and fail to follow my thought,
know that they are lost fools,
deluded by every bit of
     knowledge.

Even a man of knowledge
behaves in accord with his own
     nature;
creatures all conform to nature;
what can one do to restrain
     them?

Attraction and hatred are poised
in the object of every sense
     experience;
a man must not fall prey
to these two brigands lurking
     on his path!

Your own duty done imperfectly
is better than another man's
    done well.
It is better to die in one's own
    duty;
another man's duty is perilous.

Arjuna

Krishna, what makes a person
commit evil
against his own will,
as if compelled by force?

Lord Krishna

It is desire and anger, arising
from nature's quality of passion;
know it here as the enemy,
voracious and very evil!

As fire is obscured by smoke
and a mirror by dirt,
as an embryo is veiled by its
    caul,
so is knowledge obscured by
    this.

caul
a membrane that encloses
a fetus; it often covers the
head of a child at birth

Knowledge is obscured
by the wise man's eternal
    enemy,
which takes form as desire,
an insatiable fire, Arjuna.
The senses, mind, and
    understanding
are said to harbor desire;
with these desire obscures
    knowledge
and confounds the embodied
    self.

Therefore, first restrain
your senses, Arjuna,
then kill this evil
that ruins knowledge and
    judgment.

Men say that the senses are
    superior
to their objects, the mind
    superior to the senses,
understanding superior to the
    mind;
higher than understanding is
    the self.

Knowing the self beyond
    understanding,
sustain the self with the self.
Great warrior, kill the enemy
menacing you in the form of
    desire!

Stories of Vedanta Sages: Excerpt from *Philosophies of India*

Teachings on *Maya*, by Heinrich Zimmer

The king of the present story, who became the pupil of the philosopher Śaṅkara, was a man of sound and realistic mind who could not get over the fact of his own royal splendor and august personality. When his teacher directed him to regard all things, including the exercise of power and enjoyment of kingly pleasure, as no more than equally indifferent reflexes (purely phenomenal) of the **transcendental essence that was the Self not only of himself but of all things,** he felt some resistance. And when he was told that that one and only Self was made to seem multiple by the deluding-force of his own inborn ignorance, he determined to put his guru to the test and prove whether he would behave as a person absolutely unconcerned.

The following day, therefore, when the philosopher was coming along one of the stately approaches to the palace, to deliver his next lecture to the king, a large and dangerous elephant, maddened by heat, was let loose at him.

> **transcendental essence that was the Self not only of himself but of all things**
> According to Vedanta, the Self (Sanskrit, *Atman*) and Brahman, ultimate reality, are one and the same; this is the fundamental teaching of monism.

Śaṅkara turned and fled the moment he perceived his danger, and when the animal nearly reached his heels, disappeared from view. When he was found, he was at the top of a lofty palm tree, which he had ascended with a dexterity more usual among sailors than intellectuals. The elephant was caught, fettered, and conducted back to the stables, and the great Śaṅkara, perspiration breaking from every pore, came before his pupil.

Politely, the king apologized to the master of cryptic wisdom for the unfortunate, nearly disastrous incident; then, with a smile scarcely concealed and half pretending great seriousness, he inquired why the venerable teacher had resorted to physical flight, since he must have been aware that the elephant was of a purely illusory, phenomenal character.

The sage replied, "Indeed, in highest truth, the elephant is non-real. Nevertheless, you and I are as non-real as that elephant. Only your ignorance, clouding the truth with this spectacle of non-real phenomenality, made you see phenomenal me go up a non-real tree."

The second anecdote also turns on the undeniable physical impression made by an elephant; this time, however, the **adhikārin** is a very earnest seeker who takes precisely the opposite attitude to that of the materialistic king. Śrī Rāmakrishna used often to recite this tale to illustrate the mystery of māyā. It is an apt, surprising, and memorable example, touched with the gentle humor characteristic of so many Indian popular narratives.

adhikārin
Hindu spiritual disciple

An old guru—so we hear—was about to conclude the secret lessons that he had been giving to an advanced pupil on the omnipresence of the divine Spiritual Person. "Everything," said the wise old teacher, while his pupil listened, indrawn and full of the bliss of learning, "is God, the Infinite, pure and real, boundless and beyond the pairs of opposites, devoid of differentiating qualities and limiting distinctions. That is the final meaning of all the teachings of our holy wisdom."

The pupil understood. "God," he responded, "is the sole reality. That Divine One may be found in everything, unaffected by suffering or any fault. Every You and I is Its abode, every form an obscuring figuration within which that unique, unacting Activator dwells." He was elated: a wave of feeling swept through him tremendously, and he felt luminous and immense, like a cloud which, increasing, has come to fill the firmament. When he walked, now, it was nimbly and without weight.

Sublime, like the only cloud, in all-pervading solitude, he was walking, keeping to the middle of the road, when a huge elephant came from the opposite direction. The mahout, or driver, riding on the neck, shouted, "Clear the way," and the numerous tinkling bells of the net-covering of the great animal rang with a silvery peal to the rhythm of its soft inaudible tread. The self-exalted student of the science of Vedānta, though full of divine feeling, yet heard and saw the coming of the elephant. And he said to himself, "Why should I make way for that elephant? I am God. The elephant is God. Should God be afraid of God?" And so, fearlessly and with faith, he continued in the middle of the road. But when God came to God, the elephant swung its trunk around the waist of the thinker and tossed him out of the way. He landed hard and was a little hurt, but more greatly shocked. Covered with dust, limping, bruised, and unsettled in his mind, he returned to the teacher and recounted his confusing experience. The guru listened serenely, and when the tale was told, simply replied, "Indeed, you *are* God. So is the elephant. But why did you not listen to God's voice calling to you from the mahout, who is also God, to clear the way?"

Writings of Mohandas K. Gandhi: Excerpt from *All Men Are Brothers: Life and Thoughts of Mahatma Gandhi as Told in His Own Words*

compiled and edited by Krishna Kripalani

If we had attained the full vision of Truth, we would no longer be mere seekers, but have become one with God, for Truth is God. But being only seekers, we prosecute our quest, and are conscious of our imperfection. And if we are imperfect ourselves, religion as conceived by us must also be imperfect. We have not realized religion in its perfection, even as we have not realized God. Religion of our conception, being thus imperfect, is always subject to a process of evolution. And if all faiths outlined by men are imperfect, the question of comparative merit does not arise. All faiths constitute a revelation of Truth, but all are imperfect, and liable to error. Reverence for other faiths need not blind us to their faults. We must be keenly alive to the defects of our own faith also, yet not leave it on that account, but try to overcome those defects. Looking at all religions with an equal eye, we would not only not hesitate, but would think it our duty, to blend into our faith every acceptable feature of other faiths.

Even as a tree has a single trunk, but many branches and leaves, so there is one true and perfect Religion, but it becomes many, as it passes through the human medium. The one Religion is beyond all speech. Imperfect men put it into such language as they can command, and their words are interpreted by other men equally imperfect. Whose interpretation is to be held to be the right one? Everybody is right from his own standpoint, but it is not possible that everybody is wrong. Hence the necessity of tolerance, which does not mean indifference to one's own faith, but a more intelligent and purer love for it. Tolerance gives us spiritual insight, which is as far from fanaticism as the North Pole from the South. True knowledge of religion breaks down the barriers between faith and faith.

Yeravda Mandir a book by Gandhi, subtitled *Ashram Observances*

Yeravda Mandir, 1935

I could not live for a single second without religion. Many of my political friends despair of me because they say that even my politics are derived from religion. And they are right. My politics and all other activities of mine are derived from my religion. I go further and say that every activity of a man of religion must be derived from his religion, because religion means being bound to God, that is to say God rules your every breath.

Harijan, March 21, 1934

For me, politics bereft of religion are absolute dirt, ever to be shunned. Politics concern nations and that which concerns the welfare of nations must be one of the concerns of a man who is religiously inclined, in other words, a seeker after God and Truth. For me God and Truth are convertible terms, and if anyone told me that God was a God of untruth or a God of torture, I would decline to worship Him. Therefore in politics also we have to establish the Kingdom of Heaven.

Young India, June 18, 1925

Young India
a journal in English published by Gandhi

For Reflection

1. According to the Second Teaching of *The Bhagavad-Gita,* what are Arjuna's reasons for not wanting to fight? How does *The Bhagavad-Gita* explain the Hindu doctrine of reincarnation?

2. "Be intent on action, / not on the fruits of action" Based on your reading from *The Bhagavad-Gita,* what is intended by this teaching?

3. How does the anecdote of the elephant and its driver (mahout) illustrate the Vedanta doctrine of monism, that all is one?

4. Explain Gandhi's perspective on the variety of religions.

5. Why does Gandhi insist on the interconnection of politics and religion? How do his views compare to those of our society?

Chapter 4

Buddhism

Originating in India in the sixth century BC, Buddhism eventually spread across much of Asia. In the process three main divisions of Buddhism developed: Theravada, Mahayana, and Vajrayana, or Tibetan Buddhism. All are represented by the three primary sources included here. Important similarities among the sources reflect the basic agreement among all Buddhists with regard to essential points.

The Dhammapada is a Theravada text that is a collection of early sayings, traditionally believed to be statements of Gautama the Buddha. It has been passed down in the Pali language, an ancient Indian dialect and close relative of Sanskrit. Literally, *Dhammapada* means "sayings of the *dhamma*." *Dhamma* essentially means "Buddhist teachings." When reading the text, look for the connections among the various teachings. Meditation, for example, coupled with the avoidance of "intoxicants" (mental impurities brought about by inappropriate desires) is said to lead to "awareness," which in turn leads to the ultimate liberation of *Nibbāna* (Pali for the Sanskrit *nirvana*). References are also made in this reading to other central Buddhist teachings such as *anatta* (the doctrine denying a permanent self), the Three Jewels (the Buddha, the Dharma, and the **Saṅgha**, or Buddhist monastic community), the Four Noble Truths, and the Noble Eightfold Path. *The Dhammapada's* explanation of central teachings, believed to have been uttered by the Buddha himself, has made *The Dhammapada* very popular among all Buddhists, not only among the Theravada.

Saṅgha
the Buddhist community of monks and nuns; one of the Three Jewels of Buddhism

Zen is one among many forms of Mahayana Buddhism. Basic aspects of Zen can be discerned from its name. The Japanese *zen* is from the Chinese *ch'an*, which in turn is from the Sanskrit *dhyana*. In all three languages, the word means "meditation," the fundamental practice of Zen Buddhism. Born of a combination of Indian Buddhism and Chinese Taoism, Zen eventually emerged as a prominent Japanese form of Buddhism.

During its founding stage in China, the most important figure was Hui-neng (AD 638–713). Originally a poor boy from the hinterlands, the Fifth Patriarch of Ch'an recognized Hui-neng as being enlightened beyond all the monks. In his *Platform Sutra of the Sixth Patriarch*, Hui-neng recounts how he was named Sixth Patriarch. As the excerpt begins, the Fifth Patriarch has just announced a contest to determine who is to become the next patriarch. Note the master-disciple relationship that continues to characterize Zen to this day. In our second excerpt from the *Platform Sutra*, Hui-neng expounds basic teachings of Zen: that "perfect wisdom is inherent in all people"and that "sitting in meditation" is essential for gaining enlightenment. When reading from this portion of the *Platform Sutra*, consider how these teachings relate to those expounded in *The Dhammapada*.

Vajrayana, or Tibetan Buddhism, features among other things the belief that certain very enlightened individuals, or lamas, can control their rebirths. Reincarnated lamas are known as *tulkus*. In his autobiography *Freedom in Exile*, the Dalai Lama offers details regarding reincarnation, including his own.

Excerpts from *The Dhammapada*

Chapter II: Awareness

21. The path to **the Deathless** is awareness;
    Unawareness, the path of death.
    They who are aware do not die;
    They who are unaware are as dead.

22. Having known this distinctly,
    Those who are wise in awareness,
    Rejoice in awareness,
    Delighted in the pasture of the **noble ones.**

the Deathless
nirvana (Pali, *Nibbāna*)

noble ones
those who are on the
path to *nirvana*

23. Those meditators,
    persevering,
    Forever firm of enterprise,
    Those steadfast ones
    touch Nibbāna,
    Incomparable release from
    bonds.

24. Fame increases for the one who stands alert,
    Mindful, and of pure deeds;
    Who with due consideration acts, restrained,
    Who lives dhamma, being aware.

25. By standing alert, by awareness,
    By restraint and control too,
    The intelligent one could make an island
    That a flood does not overwhelm.

26. People deficient in wisdom, childish ones,
    Engage in unawareness.
    But the wise one guards awareness
    Like the greatest treasure.

27. Engage not in unawareness,
    Nor in intimacy with sensual delight.
    Meditating, the one who is aware
    Attains extensive ease.

28. When the wise one by awareness expels unawareness,
    Having ascended the palace of wisdom,
    He, free from sorrow, steadfast,
    The sorrowing folk observes, the childish,
    As one standing on a mountain
    [Observes] those standing on the ground below.

29. Among those unaware, the one aware,
    Among the sleepers, the wide-awake,
    The one with great wisdom moves on,
    As a racehorse who leaves behind a nag.

30. By awareness, **Maghavan**
     To supremacy among the gods arose.
>   Awareness they praise;
>   Always censured is
>   unawareness.

Maghavan
another name of the ancient Indian god Sakka, who is depicted within the Buddhist tradition as being highly favorable to the Buddha

31. The **bhikkhu** who delights
    in awareness,
    Who sees in unawareness
       the fearful,
    Goes, burning, like a fire,
    The **fetter** subtle and
       gross.

bhikku
a Buddhist monk

fetter
term used in Buddhism to refer to any one of the various mental states that bind one to *samsāra*, the wheel of rebirth

32. The bhikkhu who delights
    in awareness,
    Who sees in unawareness
       the fearful—
    He is not liable to suffer
       fall;
    In Nibbāna's presence is
       such a one.

Chapter V: The Childish

60. Long is the night for one awake,
     Long is a league to one exhausted,
     Long is *samsāra* to the childish ones
     Who know not dhamma true.

61. If while moving [through
        life], one were not to
        meet
     Someone better or like
        unto oneself,
     Then one should move
        firmly by oneself;
     There is no companion
        ship in the childish.

> **samsāra**
> for Buddhism, Hinduism, Jainism, and Sikhism, the wheel of rebirth, and the this-worldly realm of existence

62. A childish person be
        comes anxious,
     Thinking, "Sons are
        mine!
     Wealth is mine!"
     Not even a self is there [to call] one's own.
     Whence sons? Whence wealth?

> **Not even a self is there**
> reference to anatta ("no self"), the Buddhist doctrine denying a permanent self

63. A childish one who knows his childishness
     Is, for that reason, even like a wise person.
     But a childish one who thinks himself wise
     Is truly called a childish one.

64. Even though, throughout his life,
     A childish one attends on a wise person,
     He does not [thereby] perceive dhamma,
     As a ladle, the flavour of the dish.

65. Even though, for a brief moment,
     An intelligent one attends on a wise person,

He quickly perceives dhamma,
As the tongue, the flavour of the dish.

66. Childish ones, of little intelligence,
Go about with a self that is truly an enemy;
Performing the deed that is bad,
Which is of bitter fruit.

67. That deed done is not good,
Having done which, one regrets;
The consequence of which one receives,
Crying with tear-stained face.

68. But that deed done is good,
Having done which, one does not regret;
The consequence of which one receives,
With pleasure and with joy.

69. The childish one thinks it is like honey
While the bad [he has done] is not yet matured.
But when the bad [he has done] is matured,
Then the childish one comes by suffering.

70. Month by month a childish one
Might **eat food with a kusa grass blade**.

eat food with a *kusa* grass blade
The *kusa* grass blade is very thin; this refers to the limited amount of food eaten by ascetics, in contrast to the Buddhist "Middle Way" of moderation and following the teachings of the Buddha.

He is not worth a six teenth part
Of those who have understood dhamma.

71. For a bad act done does not coagulate
Like freshly extracted milk.
Burning, it follows the childish one,
Like fire concealed in ashes.

72. Only for his detriment
Does knowledge arise for the childish one.
It ruins his good fortune,
Causing his [very] head to fall.

73. He would desire unreal glory
And pre-eminence among bhikkhus,
Authority, too, concerning dwellings,
And offerings in other families.

74. "Let both householders and **those who have gone
forth**
Think that it is my work alone;
In whatever is to be done or not done,
Let them be dependent on me alone!"
Such is the thought of the childish one;
Desire and pride increase.

75. The means of acquisi-
tion is one,
And another the way
leading to Nibbāna.

**those who have gone
forth**
Buddhist monks

Having recognized this as so,
Let a bhikkhu who is a disciple of the Buddha
Not delight in [receiving] esteem;
Let him cherish disengagement.

Chapter VI: The Sagacious

76.   The one who sees one's faults,
Who speaks reprovingly, wise,
Whom one would see as an indicator of treasures,
With such a sagacious person, one would associate.
To one associating with such a person,
The better it will be, not the worse.

77.   He would counsel, instruct,
And restrain [one] from rude behaviour.
To the good, he is pleasant;
To the bad is he unpleasant.

78.   Let one not associate
With low persons, bad friends.
But let one associate
With noble persons, worthy friends.

79.   One who drinks of dhamma sleeps at ease,
With mind calmly clear.
In dhamma made known by noble ones,
The wise one constantly delights.

80.   Irrigators guide the water.
Fletchers bend the arrow shaft.

Wood the carpenters bend.
Themselves the wise ones tame.

81. Even as a solid rock
     Does not move on account of the wind,
     So are the wise not shaken
     In the face of blame and praise.

82. Even as a deep lake
     Is very clear and undisturbed,
     So do the wise become calm,
     Having heard the words of dhamma.

83. Everywhere, indeed, good persons "let go".
     The good ones do not occasion talk, hankering for
          pleasure.
     Touched now by ease and now by misery,
     The wise manifest no high and low.

84. Neither for one's own sake nor for the sake of another,
     A son would one wish, or wealth, or kingdom.
     One would not wish one's own prosperity by
          un-dhammic means.
     Such a one would be possessed of virtue,
          wisdom, dhamma.

85. Few are they among humans,
     The people who reach the **shore beyond.**
     But these other folk
     Only run along the [hither] bank.

shore beyond
Liberation, or *nirvana*, is the metaphor of crossing the river from *samsāra* to *nirvana* commonly applied in Buddhism.

86. But those who live according to dhamma—
In dhamma well proclaimed—
Those people will reach the shore beyond.
The realm of death is hard to cross.

87. Having forsaken a shadowy dhamma,
The wise one would cultivate the bright,
Having come from familiar abode to no abode
In disengagement, hard to relish.

88. There he would wish for delight,
Having discarded sensual desires—he who has nothing.
The wise one would purify himself
Of the defilements of the mind.

factors of enlightenment
seven qualities or mental abilities necessary for traversing the path to liberation

intoxicants
mental impurities brought about by inappropriate desires

89. Whose mind is fully well cultivated in the **factors of enlightenment,**
Who, without clinging, delight in the rejection of grasping,
Lustrous ones, who have destroyed **intoxicants,**
They have, in [this] world, attained Nibbāna.

Chapter XIV: The Awakened One

179. Whose victory is not turned into defeat,
     Whose victory no one in this world reaches,
     That **Awakened One** whose range is limitless,
     Him, the trackless, by
          what track will you
          lead?

> **Awakened One**
> a buddha; Buddhists
> believe Gautama is one
> in an infinitely long line
> of buddhas

180. For whom craving there
          is not, the netlike, the
          clinging,
     To lead him wheresoever,
     That Awakened One whose range is limitless,
     Him, the trackless, by what track will you lead?

181. Those who are intent on meditating, the wise ones,
     Delighting in the calm of going out,
     Even gods long for them,
     The Fully Enlightened Ones, the mindful.

182. Difficult is the attainment of the human state.
     Difficult the life of mortals.
     Difficult is the hearing of dhamma true.
     Difficult the appearance of Awakened Ones.

183. Refraining from all that is detrimental,
     The attainment of what is wholesome,
     The purification of one's mind:
     This is the instruction of Awakened Ones.

184. Forbearing patience is the highest austerity;
    Nibbāna is supreme, the Awakened Ones say.
    One who has gone forth is not one who hurts another,
    No harasser of others is a recluse.

185. No faultfinding, no hurting, restraint in the *pātimokkha,*
    Knowing the measure regarding food, solitary bed and
        chair,
    Application, too, of higher perception:
    This is the instruction of the Awakened Ones.

186. Not even with a rain of golden coins
    Is contentment found among sensual pleasures.
    "Sensual pleasures are of little delight, are a misery."
    Knowing so, the wise one

187. Takes no delight
    Even for heavenly sensual pleasures.
    One who delights in the ending of craving
    Is a disciple of the Fully Enlightened One.

188. Many for refuge go
    To mountains and to forests,
    To shrines that are groves or trees—
    Humans who are threatened by fear.

pātimokkha
summary of rules govern-
ing Buddhist monastic
life

189. This is not a refuge secure,
     This refuge is not the highest.
     Having come to this refuge,
     One is not released from all misery.

190. But who to the Buddha, Dhamma,
     And Saṅgha as refuge has gone,
     Sees with full insight
     The Four Noble Truths;

191. Misery, the arising of misery,
     And the transcending of misery,
     The Noble Eightfold Path
     Leading to the allaying of misery.

192. This, indeed, is a refuge secure.
     This is the highest refuge.
     Having come to this refuge,
     One is released from all misery.

193. Hard to come by is a person of nobility;
     Not everywhere is he born.
     Wherever that wise one is born,
     That family prospers in happiness.

194. Joyful is the arising of Awakened Ones.
     Joyful, the teaching of Dhamma true.
     Joyful, too, the concord of the Saṅgha.
     Joyful, the austere practice of those in concord.

195. Of one worshipping those worthy of worship,
    Whether Awakened Ones or disciples,
    Who have transcended preoccupying tendencies,
    Crossed over grief and lamentation,

196. Of one worshipping such as them,
    Calmed ones who fear nothing,
    The merit cannot be quantified
    By anyone saying, "It is of this extent."

Zen Buddhism: Excerpt from *A Source Book in Chinese Philosophy:* "The Platform Sutra of the Sixth Patriarch"

6. . . . At midnight **Head Monk Shen-hsiu,** holding a candle, wrote a verse on the wall of the south corridor, without anyone knowing about it, which said:

Head Monk Shen-hsiu

a celebrated Zen master who emphasized the method of gradual awakening (see "method of sudden enlightenment" below)

The body is the tree of perfect wisdom (*bodhi*)
The mind is the stand of a bright mirror.
At all times diligently wipe it.
Do not allow it to become dusty.

7. . . . The **Fifth Patriarch** said, "The verse you wrote shows some but not complete understanding. You have arrived at the front door but you have not yet entered it. Ordinary people, by practicing in accordance with your verse, will not fail. But it is futile to seek the supreme perfect wisdom while holding to such a view. One must enter the door and see his own nature. Go away and come back after thinking a day or two. Write another verse and present it to me. If then you have entered the door and have seen your own nature, I will give you the **robe and the Law**." Head Monk Shen-hsiu went away and for several days could not produce another verse.

8. . . . I (Hui-neng) also composed a verse. . . . My verse says:

> Fundamentally perfect wisdom has no tree.
> Nor has the bright mirror any stand.
> Buddha-nature is forever clear and pure.
> Where is there any dust?

Fifth Patriarch
according to its own tradition, Zen Buddhism began in India at the time of the Buddha, who transmitted the subtle truths of Zen to a follower who established a line of Zen patriarchs; Bodhidharma, the twenty-eighth in this line of Indian patriarchs, is said to have brought Zen to China about AD 520, thus becoming the first in a separate line of Chinese patriarchs, the fifth of whom was Hung-jen (the "Fifth Patriarch" in Hui-neng's narrative)

robe and the Law
symbols of the position of Patriarch; "the Law" relates back to the dharma, or the teachings of the Buddha

Another verse, which says:

The mind is the tree of perfect wisdom.
The body is the stand of a bright mirror.
The bright mirror is originally clear and pure.
Where has it been defiled by any dust?

Monks in the hall were all surprised at these verses. I, however, went back to the rice-pounding area. The Fifth Patriarch suddenly realized that I alone had the good knowledge and understanding of the basic idea, but he was afraid lest the rest learn it. He therefore told them, "He does not understand perfectly after all."

9. The Fifth Patriarch waited till midnight, called me to come to the hall, and expounded the *Diamond Scripture.* As soon as I heard this, I understood. That night the Law was imparted to me without anyone's knowing it, and thus the **method of sudden enlightenment** and the robe were transmitted to me. "You are now the Sixth Patriarch. This robe is the testimony of transmission from generation to generation. As to the Law, it is to be transmitted from mind to mind. Let people achieve enlightenment through their own effort." . . .

Diamond Scripture
Possibly the most popular Buddhist text in China, it emphasizes the mind rather than ultimate reality.

method of sudden enlightenment
To this day there are two main schools of Zen Buddhism: sudden enlightenment or awakening (Rinzai) and gradual awakening (Soto); Hui-neng is credited with having founded the school of sudden awakening, which continues to be the more prominent of the two.

Great Master Hui-neng declared, "Good and learned friends, perfect wisdom is inherent in all people. It is only because they are deluded in their minds that they cannot attain enlightenment by themselves. They must seek the help of good and learned friends of high standing to show them the way to see [their own] nature. Good and learned friends, as soon as one is enlightened, he attains wisdom." . . .

18. "Good and learned friends, according to this method sitting in meditation is at bottom neither looking at the mind nor looking at purity. Nor do we say that there should be imperturbability. Suppose we say to look at the mind. The mind is at bottom false. Since being false is the same as being illusory, there is nothing to look at. Suppose we say to look at purity. Man's nature is originally pure. It is by false thoughts that **True Thusness** is obscured. Our original nature is pure as long as it is free from false thoughts. If one does not realize that his own nature is originally pure and makes up his mind to look at purity, he is creating a false purity. Such purity has no objective existence. Hence we know that what is looked at is false. Purity has neither physical form nor character, but some people set up characters of purity and say that this is the object of our task. People who take this view hinder their own original nature and become bound by purity. If those who cultivate imperturbability would ignore people's mistakes and defects, their nature would not be perturbed. Deluded people may not be perturbed physically themselves, but whenever they speak, they

> **True Thusness**
> (Sanskrit, *tathata*; Chinese, *chen-ju*) also translated as "Suchness" or "True Reality," the ultimate ground of being, uncaused, unchangeable, and eternal

the Way

Tao, a fundamental concept in Chinese religious philosophy

criticize others and thus violate **the Way.** Thus looking at the mind or at purity causes a hindrance to the Way."

19. "Now, this being the case, in this method, what is meant by sitting in meditation? In this method, to sit means to be free from all obstacles, and externally not to allow thoughts to rise from the mind over any sphere of objects. To meditate means to realize the imperturbability of one's original nature. What is meant by meditation and calmness? Meditation means to be free from all characters externally; calmness means to be unperturbed internally. If there are characters outside and the inner mind is not disturbed, one's original nature is naturally pure and calm. It is only because of the spheres of objects that there is contact, and contact leads to perturbation. There is calmness when one is free from characters and is not perturbed. There is meditation when one is internally undisturbed. Meditation and calmness mean that external meditation is attained and internal calmness is achieved. . . ."

Tibetan Buddhism: Excerpt from *Freedom in Exile: The Autobiography of the Dalai Lama*

by Tenzin Gyatso

When I was not quite three years old, a search party that had been sent out by the Government to find the new incarnation of the Dalai Lama arrived at **Kumbum monastery.** It had been led there by a number of signs. One of these concerned the embalmed body of my predecessor, Thupten Gyatso, the **Thirteenth Dalai Lama,** who had died aged fifty-seven in 1933. During his period of sitting in state, the head was discovered to have turned from facing south to north-east. Shortly after that the Regent, himself a senior lama, had a vision. Looking into the waters of the sacred lake, Lhamoi Lhatso, in southern Tibet, he clearly saw the Tibetan letters *Ah, Ka* and *Ma* float into view. These were

Kumbum monastery
Tibetan monastery in the province of Amdo, near the city of Xining

Thirteenth Dalai Lama
The current Dalai Lama is the fourteenth in a line of incarnations of Avalokiteshvara (the Sanskrit term; in Tibetan, Chenrezig) bodhisattva of compassion (a bodhisattva is a future Buddha who, having experienced enlightenment, opts not to enter nirvana in order to assist others in their spiritual quests).

followed by the image of a monastery with a turquoise and gold roof and a path running from it to a hill. Finally, he saw a small house with strangely shaped guttering. He was sure that the letter *Ah* referred to Amdo, the north-eastern province, so it was there that the search party was sent.

By the time they reached Kumbum, the members of the search party felt that they were on the right track. It seemed likely that if the letter *Ah* referred to Amdo, then *Ka* must indicate the monastery at Kumbum—which was indeed three storeyed and turquoise roofed. They now only needed to locate a hill and a house with peculiar guttering. So they began to search the neighbouring villages. When they saw the gnarled branches of juniper wood on the roof of my parents' house, they were certain that the new Dalai Lama would not be far away. Nevertheless, rather than reveal the purpose of their visit, the group asked only to stay the night. The leader of the party, Kewtsang Rinpoché, then pretended to be a servant and spent much of the evening observing and playing with the youngest child in the house.

The child recognised him and called out "Sera Lama, Sera Lama." Sera was Kewtsang Rinpoché's monastery. Next day they left—only to return a few days later as a formal deputation. This time they brought with them a number of things that had belonged to my predecessor, together with several similar items that did not. In every case, the infant correctly identified those belonging to the Thirteenth Dalai Lama saying, "It's mine. It's mine." This more or less convinced the search party that they had found the new incarnation. However, there was another candidate to be seen before a final decision could be reached. But it was not long before the boy from Taktser was acknowledged to be the new Dalai Lama. I was that child. . . .

Actually, the business of identifying *tulkus* is more logical than it may at first appear. Given the Buddhist belief that the principle of rebirth is fact, and given that the whole purpose of reincarnation is to enable a being to continue its efforts on behalf of all suffering sentient beings, it stands to reason that it should be possible to identify individual cases. This enables them to be educated and placed in the world so that they can continue their work as soon as possible.

Mistakes in this identification process can certainly be made, but the lives of the great majority of *tulkus* (of whom there are presently a few hundred known, although in Tibet before the Chinese invasion there were probably a few thousand) are adequate testimony of its efficacy.

As I have said, the whole purpose of reincarnation is to facilitate the continuity of a being's work. This fact has great implications when it comes to searching for the successor of a particular person. For example, whilst my efforts in general are directed towards helping all sentient beings, in particular they are directed towards helping my fellow Tibetans. There-fore, if I die before Tibetans regain their freedom, it is only logical to assume that I will be born outside Tibet. Of course, it could be that by then my people will have no use for a Dalai Lama, in which case they will not bother to search for me. So I might take rebirth as an insect, or an animal—whatever would be of most value to the largest number of sentient beings.

The way that the identification process is carried out is also less mysterious than might be imagined. It begins as a simple process of elimination. Say, for instance, we are look-ing for the reincarnation of a particular monk. First it must be established when and where that monk died. Then,

considering that the new incarnation will usually be conceived a year or so after the death of its predecessor—these
lengths of time we know from experience—a timetable is
drawn up. Thus, if Lama X dies in year Y, his next incarnation
will probably he born around eighteen months to two years
later. In the year Y plus five, the child is likely to be between
three and four years old: the field has narrowed already.

For Reflection

1. Explain in your own words the teachings of *The Dham-
    mapada* on awareness. What is it, and what are its
    benefits?

2. Based on your reading of "The Awakened One" (chap-
    ter XIV of *The Dhammapada*), identify the Three Jewels
    (or Refuges). Also identify and explain the Four Noble
    Truths.

3. Compare Hui-neng's verses with Head Monk Shen-
    hsiu's verse. Why do you think Hui-neng was deter-
    mined by the Fifth Patriarch to be more enlightened?

4. Interpret in your own words Hui-neng's description of
    "sitting in meditation." What would be the likely effects
    of such practice? Do you know of similar practices in
    modern society?

5. How does the Tibetan Buddhist belief in reincarnation,
    as explained by the Dalai Lama, correlate with other
    Buddhist teachings in this chapter?

Chapter 5

Sikhism

The word *Sikhism* is derived from the Hindi *sikh*, which means "learner" or "disciple." Sikhs are disciples of the Guru—a term with three interrelated meanings. The first meaning refers to the religion's founder, Guru Nanak (1469–1539), and his nine successor Gurus, who are the ten historical leaders of Sikhism. The second meaning refers to the Adi Granth, Sikhism's sacred text, also commonly called the Guru Granth Sahib. In the year of his death, Gobind Singh (1666–1708), the tenth historical Guru, installed the Adi Granth as Guru. In its third meaning, Guru is a name for God. In all three cases, the Guru is a revealer of truth to the Sikhs.

Our first primary source in this chapter illustrates a traditional Sikh understanding of the life and characteristics of Guru Nanak. The excerpts come from a category of texts known as *janam-sakhis*, collections of stories about Sikhism's founding figure. Our excerpts include episodes from various periods and events spanning Nanak's lifetime, from his birth and childhood in the village of Talvandi, near Lahore, Pakistan, to his death seventy years later. Note the supernatural elements of Nanak's biography. The *janam-sakhis* stop short, however, of depicting Nanak as divine. He is presented as an extraordinary man with special gifts, but as merely human nonetheless. In both spiritual and worldly pursuits, Nanak is said to have surpassed his contemporaries. Note also how Guru Nanak earns the admiration of both Hindus and Muslims and how he manages to bridge their differences through his teachings and deeds.

The second reading for this chapter is the *Japjî*. The *Japjî*, composed by Guru Nanak and included at the beginning of the Adi Granth, is regularly chanted by Sikhs upon rising in the morning. The opening five lines comprise the *Mool Mantra*, a summation of Sikh theology, describing God as one, eternal, "the Creator," and "self-existent." Sikh theology is thus similar to the monotheism of Islam, even while the means of knowing God through meditative contemplation are more in keeping with Hinduism. Strive also to identify other aspects familiar to Hinduism, such as belief in rebirth.

Through the centuries since its founding, Sikhism has been mainly a religion of the Punjab region of northwestern India and eastern Pakistan, home to the ten historical Gurus and their disciples and now home to the majority of the world's twenty-three million Sikhs. But Sikhism also has become a global religion. Rev. Wadhawa Singh, originally from the Indian state of Punjab, is the religious advisor of a Sikh *gurdwara*, or house of worship, in northern California. His book *The Self Spirit* was originally published in the Punjabi language in the 1960s. Recently it has been published in English and is available to readers in North America. Both author and book thus parallel Sikhism itself as it has spread globally. The excerpt included here involves Reverend Singh's attempt to teach the subtle truths of Sikh theology to his grandson in Modesto, California. When reading this passage, try to make sense of the idea that the individual's self ultimately is identifiable with the divine, all-pervading Self Spirit.

Excerpt from *Textual Sources for the Study of Sikhism:* Events in the Life of Guru Nanak

The Birth and Childhood of Nanak

Baba Nanak was born in **Talvandi,** the son of Kalu, who was a **Bedi Khatri by caste.** In this Age of Darkness he proclaimed the **divine Name** and founded his community of followers, the **Panth.** Baba Nanak was born in the year S.1526 on the third day of the month of Vaisakh [AD April 15,1469]. He was born during the moonlit hours of early morning, that time of fragrant peace which is the **last watch of the night.** Celestial music resounded in heaven. A mighty host of gods hailed his birth, and with them all manner of spirit and divinity. "God

Baba
(Punjabi, "father") a title of respect

Talvandi
a town located in Pakistan about forty-five miles west of Lahore now bearing the name Nankana Sahib

Bedi Khatri by caste
Khatri is the Punjabi equivalent of the Sanskrit *Kshatriya,* which is the warrior class within the traditional caste system; Bedi Khatri is the name of a subcaste.

has come to save the world!" they cried.

At the time of the birth Kalu Bedi was residing in Talvandi and Nanak was actually born in the village. As he grew older he began to play with other children, but his attitude differed from theirs in that he paid heed to the spiritual things of God. When he turned five he began to give utterance to deep and mysterious thoughts. Whatever he uttered was spoken with profound understanding, with the result that everyone's doubts and questions were resolved. The Hindus vowed that a god had taken birth in human form. The Muslims declared that a follower of divine truth had been born.

When Baba Nanak turned seven his father told him that he must begin his schooling. Kalu took him to a teacher and directed him to teach the child. This the teacher agreed to do. He wrote on a wooden slate and Nanak studied with him for a single day. The following day, however, he remained silent. "Why are you not studying?" the teacher asked him. "What is it that you have studied and wish to teach me?" responded Nanak. "I have studied everything. From accountancy to the sacred scriptures, I have studied them all," answered the teacher. "These subjects which you have studied are all useless," declared Nanak. He then sang a hymn in the measure *Sini Rag* . . . [Having heard the hymn and Nanak's explanation of its meaning] the teacher was astounded and did obeisance. Acknowledging that the child had already attained perfection he said, "Do what you believe to be right."

The Call to Preach

When Nanak reached **Sultanpur** he was warmly welcomed by **Jai Ram.** Taking him to the **Nawab** his brother-in-law declared him to be a most industrious worker and asked that he might be given employment. The Nawab put him in charge of his stores. Baba Nanak duly took his seat in the **commissariat** and gave complete satisfaction to all who needed supplies. Someone reported that Nanak was indulging in misappropriation, but when Nawab Daulat Khan came to investigate the allegation he discovered that everything had actually doubled in quantity. "My steward is remarkably conscientious," he said, heaping praise on Nanak.

After returning home in the evening Baba Nanak would devote his nights to singing hymns, and when it came to the last watch of the night he would go to the river and bathe. One morning,

Sultanpur
a town in the Punjab where Nanak's elder sister Nanaki lived

Jai Ram
an official at Sultanpur who was married to Nanaki, Nanak's sister

Nawab
Nawab Daulat Khan, the local governor under whom Jai Ram served

commissariat
a food supply station

having gone to bathe, he entered the waters of the **Vein stream** but failed to emerge. His servant looked for him until mid-morning and then taking his clothes returned home to tell Jai Ram what had happened. "During the last watch of the night Nanak went into the stream to bathe," he said, "but he has not emerged." When he heard this news Jai Ram was greatly disturbed and went to the Nawab to report what had happened. The Nawab sent for nets and a thorough search was made, but to no avail.

Eventually, however, Baba Nanak did return. After three days and three nights had passed he emerged from the stream, and having done so he declared: "There is neither Hindu nor Muslim." When the Nawab heard that Nanak had reappeared and that he was speaking in this manner he sent a servant to request an interview on his behalf. Baba Nanak went to the delighted Nawab who treated him with great deference.

Panja Sahib

While travelling to **Kashmir** the Guru came to the high hill which rises above the town of **Hasan Abdal,** approximately twenty **kos** from the Indus river. While he was resting near the town his companion **Mardana** became thirsty.

Mardana asked the Guru for water but there was none to be found in the vicinity. When the thirsty Mardana became increasingly agitated the Guru said to him: "At the top of that high hill there lives a Muslim **faqir** called Vali Qandhari. He has water close at hand, but nowhere else in this area will you find it. Go and ask him for some of his water. When he sees that you look like a Muslim, he will probably let you have some."

Mardana accepted the Guru's advice and set off to quench his thirst. With much difficulty he struggled up the hill and found Vali Qandhari sitting at the top. Beside him was a natural basin in which he stored water for his own use. Mardana told him that he was thirsty and politely asked for water. Observing his appearance and foreign dress, Vali Qandhari asked him, "Where have you come from, thirsty fellow? What is your name and what brings you here? Are you alone or is there someone with you?"

Kashmir
historical region in northwestern India and northeastern Pakistan

Hasan Abdal
a town in Pakistan, located between Peshawar and Rawalpindi; important for Sikhism due to the event narrated here

kos
a unit of distance, variably measuring between one and three miles

Mardana
a Muslim bard or minstrel and friend of Guru Nanak who accompanied Nanak on his travels

faqir
(Arabic, "a poor man") a Muslim ascetic

pir
a Muslim term of respect for a religious teacher or authority

"I have come with Guru Nanak, the celebrated holy man of the Punjab," answered Mardana. "He it is whom the Hindus regard as their guru and Muslims as their **pir.** Having travelled the entire world reclaiming lost souls he is now on his way to Kashmir. He is resting at the bottom of the hill. I am his minstrel companion and my name is Mardana the Bard. I accompany the Guru wherever he goes and sing his hymns."

Vali Qandhari was furious when he heard the Guru praised in this manner. Burning with anger, he said to Mardana, "If your holy man is so marvellous why doesn't he use his powers to produce water down there where he is sitting? One ought to give water to a thirsty person, but I'm certainly not giving any to you. Go back to your holy man and tell him to produce water for you. Let *him* be the one who quenches your thirst."

The dejected Mardana tramped down the hill and told the Guru what had happened. "When he was told how important you are Vali Qandhari became very upset and refused to give me any water," he said. Having heard what had happened, the Guru smiled. "Muslims like their fellow Muslims," he said. "Approach him humbly and bring some water back."

[Mardana returned] to him with humble courtesy. "I am your fellow Muslim," he said, "and you possess great powers. Please give me some water so that I may satisfy my thirst." Vali Qandhari angrily responded, "Here you are writhing in anguish and that holy man Nanak, for all his supernatural skills, is unable to help you! Leave him and you will have water."

Mandana returned to the Guru thoroughly upset. "He won't give me any water," he wailed, "and here I am dying of thirst." The Guru could read the inner thoughts of others and he knew what was in Vali Qandhari's heart. To quench Mardana's thirst he picked up a piece of wood and struck the ground at the foot of the hill. Instantly there appeared a spring of cool, clear water. At the same time Vali Qandhari's little reservoir of water sank into the hill and disappeared. Not a drop remained.

Overwhelmed with fear and anger, Vali Qandhari used his prodigious strength to send a huge boulder tumbling down the hill to where the Guru was sitting. Down it hurtled, crushing everything in its path. When he saw it descending on him the Guru raised his hand and stopped it in its tracks. As he did so his hand sank into the boulder leaving an imprint in the rock. Vali Qandhari, having witnessed the Guru open a spring of limpid water and then stop a boulder with his hand, was totally abashed. Humbly he acknowledged the Guru's mighty powers and, falling at his feet, begged for his blessing. The Guru responded affectionately. He urged the penitent Vali Qandhari to put aside his pride and having brought him peace he proceeded on his way.

The Death of Baba Nanak

Guru Baba Nanak then went and sat under a withered acacia which immediately produced leaves and flowers, becoming verdant again. **Guru Angad** prostrated himself. Baba Nanak's wife began to weep and the various members of his family joined her in her grief . . . The assembled congregation sang hymns of praise and Baba Nanak passed into an ecstatic trance. While thus transported, and in obedience to the divine will, he sang the hymn entitled *The Twelve Months*. It was early morning and the time had come for his final departure . . . His sons asked him, "What will happen to us?" The Guru reassured them. "Even the Guru's dogs lack nothing, my sons," he said. "You shall be abundantly supplied with food and clothing, and if you repeat the Guru's name you will be liberated from the bondage of human life."

Hindus and Muslims who had put their faith in the divine Name began to debate what should be done with the Guru's corpse. "We shall bury him," said the Muslims. "No, let us cremate his body," said the Hindus. "Place flowers on both sides of my body," said Baba Nanak, "flowers from the Hindus on the right side and flowers from the Muslims on the left. If tomorrow the Hindus' flowers are still fresh let my body be burned, and if the Muslims' flowers are still fresh let it be buried."

Guru Angad
a friend of Nanak and his successor, and thus the second historical Guru of Sikhism

Kirtan Sohila* and *Arati
Sikh hymns

Baba Nanak then commanded the congregation to sing. They sang ***Kirtan Sohila*** and ***Arati*** . . . Baba Nanak then covered himself with a sheet and passed away. Those who had gathered around him prostrated themselves, and when the sheet was removed they found that there was nothing under it. The flowers on both sides remained fresh, and both Hindus and Muslims took their respective shares. All who were gathered there prostrated themselves again.

Excerpt from *Sikhism: The Japjî,* the Sikh Morning Prayer

Japjî is the only work recorded in the Adi Granth which is not intended to be sung. Instead it is chanted.

The Basic Credal Statement (Mūl Mantra)
There is one Supreme Being, the Eternal Reality, the Creator, without fear and devoid of enmity, immortal, never incarnated,
self-existent, known by grace through the Guru.
The Eternal One, from the beginning, through all time, present
now, the Everlasting Reality.

1. Never can you be known through ritual purity though one cleanse oneself a hundred thousand times. Never can you be revealed by silent reflection though one dwell absorbed in the deepest meditation. Though one gather vast riches the hunger remains, no cunning will help in the hereafter. How then is Truth to be attained, how the veil of falsehood torn aside? Nanak, thus it is written: Submit to the divine Order, walk in its way.

2. Though all that exists is its visible expression, the divine Order is far beyond all describing. All forms of life are created by it, and it alone can determine who is great. Some

are exalted, some abased; some must suffer while others find joy. Some receive blessing, others are condemned, doomed by the divine Order to endless transmigration. All are within it, none can evade it. They, Nanak, who truly comprehend it renounce their blind self-centred pride.

3. They who are strong sing of the Supreme One's might; they who receive gifts sing of grace. Some acclaim majesty and wonders performed; others from their learning discern wisdom to be praised. Some praise power made manifest in creation, how life is raised up, cast down, and reincarnated anew. Some sing of distance, of dwelling afar; others of presence, immanent in all creation. Countless the number who tell of the Supreme One, describing in endless ways. None can ever hope to succeed, for none can encompass infinity. Continual the giving with endless gifts, caring for us and endlessly supplying our needs. The divine Order it is that directs our path. For ever joyous is the Divine One, Nanak, for ever free from care.

4. The Eternal One whose Name is Truth speaks to us in infinite love. Insistently we beg for the gifts which are by grace bestowed. What can we offer in return for all this goodness? What gift will gain entrance to the hallowed Court? What words can we utter to attract this love? At the ambrosial hour of fragrant dawn meditate on the grandeur of the one true Name. Past actions determine the nature of our birth, but grace alone reveals the door to liberation. See the Divine Spirit, Nanak, dwelling immanent in all. Know the Divine Spirit as the One, the eternal, the changeless Truth.

5. Futile it is to make and install an idol, a mere figure of the Supreme One who is devoid of spot or stain. Whoever serves wins honour, Nanak, so sing of the Supreme One,

of boundless excellence. Sing praises, hear them sung, and nourish love within your heart. Thus shall your suffering all be banished and peace take its place within. The Guru's Word is the mystic sound, the voice of the scriptures immanent in all. **Shiva, Vishnu, Brahma and Parvati, all are but manifestations of the one divine Guru.** Were my mind to comprehend the Eternal One my words would surely fail.

One thing only I ask of the Guru. May the Gracious One, the Giver of all, constantly dwell in my thoughts and recollection.

6. I should bathe at a pilgrimage spot if that would give you pleasure. Without your blessing nothing is obtained. Throughout all creation nothing can be gained except by means of your divine grace. The person who accepts but a single word from the Guru shall find within a treasure trove of jewels. Let me never forget that single perception, the constant remembrance of the Giver of all.

7. If one were to live through all **four ages (yuga)** or even ten times their span; if one were to be famed throughout the world,

Shiva, Vishnu, Brahma and Parvati, all are but manifestations of the one divine Guru
four prominent Hindu gods; the idea that they are manifestations of the Guru (here, this means God) shows similarity with the Hindu doctrine of monism—that all, including the gods and goddesses, is ultimately one

four ages (yuga)
Sikhism espouses a cyclical time scheme, with each cycle of time divided into four eras (Sanskrit, yugas), each consisting of many thousands of years.

acknowledged as leader by all; if one were to earn an exalted name and a glory which covered the earth, without your
blessing all would be futile. If your gracious glance avoids
such a person all turn their faces away. Lowest of worms,
scorned and blamed by all! The worthless are converted to
virtue, Nanak, and to the virtuous you impart yet more. You
alone have the power so to do; no one confers virtue on
you.

8. By listening to the Word one gathers all the qualities of the spiritually adept. By listening to the Word one
comprehends the deepest mysteries of the universe. When
one listens to the Word the vastness of the world comes
into view, its continents, its realms, and under it the nether
regions. If one listens to the Word the power of Death is
overcome. The devout, declares Nanak, dwell in everlasting
bliss, for suffering and sin must flee from all who hear the
Word.

Excerpt from *The Self Spirit*

by Wadhawa Singh

1

I was at home with my family and grandchildren when my
grandson Sukhdeep Singh, 14 years old at the time, asked
me, "Nana Ji [Dear Grandfather], what is *Aatma* [the Self
Spirit]?" I was quite surprised at his question because the
subject is more naturally suited for grownups and mature
individuals. Nonetheless, I felt it my obligation to satisfy his
curiosity with an adequate response. I said, "Son, *Aatma*—

the Self Spirit—is not a physical body but a living entity in the body that enables it to think, walk and talk. It is also the creator of the entire universe, both seen and unseen, being a particle of an indivisible, all-pervasive God: *Parmatma*—the Universal Spirit. The Universal Spirit in the form of the Self Spirit operates this universe through the vehicles of physical forms. In order to experience an illustration of this, close your eyes. Your body will no longer be visible and gradually you will cease to feel its presence. Now, try to understand what you are without it." Sukhdeep Singh closed his eyes and after a couple of minutes told me, "Nana Ji, I feel that I am a living being. Even though I don't see anything, I realize this through my consciousness coming forth from my invisible living self." I told him, "This very existence of yours is the *Aatma*—the Personal Self, the Self Spirit. When it is undeveloped, it has limited awareness, but when it is fully developed, it blossoms and transforms into pristine Universal Spirit, the Supreme God."

2

It is a misconception that our being is made of flesh and blood. Our being—the Self Spirit—is subtle and all pervasive and can maintain itself separately from our material self. It exists everywhere, as if it were a mind or consciousness in itself and in fact it is precisely that. I asked Sukhdeep Singh to close his eyes again. We were at home in Modesto, California (USA) and I instructed him to go to the front door of his home in Model Town, Hoshiarpur (India). He reported, "Nana Ji, I have arrived there." I further instructed him to enter the house by opening the door if it was closed. He responded, "Nana Ji, I am in the living room now." I asked him to sit down in a chair to which he replied, "Nana Ji, I am sitting in a chair." I asked him to call his grandmother if she was around, but he didn't see her. However, he reassured me that he was definitely sitting in the living room of his residence in Hos[h]iarpur. At this my other grandchildren, Suk[h]deep's brothers and sisters, all spoke in unison. "Nana Ji, he is lying. He is present here. Look at his body right here." Sukhdeep Singh responded, "No, No, Nana Ji, though my body is in California, my mind—the real conscious self—is in Hoshiarpur." Had Sukhdeep Singh been a bit more enlightened he could have even seen his grandma. He loves her so dearly that he would have been lost in conversation with her and for a while would have totally forgotten about his physical self in California.

3

In our initial stage of existence, prior to advancing spiritually through purification, our being has the form of thoughts, feelings, and emotions, which are good and bad, divine and worldly of all kinds. This is our individual self, or soul, perceptible though not yet visible. The purification of this mind starts through engaging with the teachings of Guru. When the soul or individual self is completely purified it becomes the spiritual self and is known as the Self Spirit. Here the divine light *(Jot)* has blossomed and is made manifest in our perception. By its further ascension it becomes the Universal Spirit. The Universal Spirit is the real and eternal home of divine knowledge.

For Reflection

1. Summarize the birth narrative of Guru Nanak, noting the supernatural events that are said to have occurred. How does his birth narrative compare to those of other religious figures about whom you are familiar (such as Jesus of Nazareth or Gautama the Buddha)?

2. The *janam-sakhis* report that when Guru Nanak was born, Hindus "vowed that a god had taken birth in human form" and Muslims "declared that a follower of divine truth had been born." Based on what you know about these two religions, try to explain their differing interpretations of the nature of Guru Nanak.

3. In three or four sentences, and in your own words, describe the nature of God according to the *Mool Mantra* (the first five lines of the *Japjī*).

4. *Aatma*, the Self Spirit; *Parmatma*, the Universal Spirit: explain the relationship between these two concepts, which are fundamental to Wadhawa Singh's attempt to teach spiritual truths to his grandson.

Chapter 6

Confucianism

K'ung Fu-tzu (551–479 BC), better known in Western culture as Confucius, is one of the world's most influential people. Confucianism, the religious and philosophical tradition that stems from his teachings, has for centuries been a foundational worldview of peoples throughout East Asia. This is all quite remarkable, given that Confucius seems to have died thinking himself a failure. The integrity and wisdom of his teachings, however, enabled them to endure, and eventually, in the second century BC, to be adopted as an official philosophy of China.

Most of what is known about Confucius comes to us from *The Analects*, a collection of sayings of Confucius that his followers assembled after his death. There are twenty-two books in *The Analects*. To provide a sense of the diversity within a given book, our excerpt includes all of Book II. Also included are specific selections from books in *The Analects* that address three important points of emphasis of Confucius's teachings.

The first is the concept of *jen*, also known as "goodness," "love," or (as in this translation) "benevolence." For Confucius, *jen* is the supreme virtue and the essential basis for sound interpersonal relationships. As the sections cited here infer, holding fast to *jen* is empowering but is not necessarily easy to do.

The second teaching is *li. Li* refers in a narrow sense to sacred rites. More generally, *li* means "proper behavior." Confucius intends both meanings together; one ought to behave properly, *as if* performing sacred rites.

The third point of emphasis, not reducible to just one term, is learning. Confucius, himself a devoted student of classical Chinese culture, promoted learning as the crucial means to becoming a virtuous person. When reading the excerpts from *The Analects*, look for the interconnections between *jen, li,* and learning.

"The Great Learning" itself, not including the several pages of ancient commentary that commonly are included in modern editions, is about only one page long (all of which is included here). But the short length belies its vast significance for the Confucian tradition. Often described as a concise summary of the basic teachings, "The Great Learning" sets forth the Confucian understanding of the harmony of relationships that connect the individual to the society. Just as "branches" depend on "roots," so too do healthy social relationships depend on the soundness of an individual's virtue. Note how the process of learning, which Confucius greatly emphasizes, plays a pivotal role here.

Herbert Fingarette's *Confucius: The Secular as Sacred* shows how Confucius's teachings, most especially his teachings on *li*, or sacred rites, have modern relevance. Fingarette describes *li* as the means by which humans are transformed from mere biological creatures to civilized beings. Unlike *jen*, which is innate, the various "rites" of *li* are learned and are performed spontaneously—for example, as we shake hands when politely offering greetings. Readers of Fingarette's interpretation of *li* are challenged to compare their own experiences of learning how to be a virtuous person.

Excerpts from *The Analects*

by Confucius

(The Analects) Book II
Standard reference to sayings of *The Analects* is made by identifying book and saying numbers—for example, 2:1 refers to the first passage in our excerpts.

the Master
The actual Chinese name from which we get Confucius is K'ung Fu-tzu, which means "Master K'ung"; English translations of *The Analects* commonly refer to him as "the Master," his honorific title.

BOOK II

1. **The Master** said, "The rule of virtue can be compared to the Pole Star which commands the homage of the multitude of stars, without leaving its place."

2. The Master said, "The Odes are three hundred in number. They can be summed up in one phrase,
Swerving not from the right path."

3. The Master said, "Guide them by edicts, keep them in line with punishments, and the common people will stay out of trouble but will have no sense of shame. Guide them

by virtue, keep them in line with the rites, and they will, besides having a sense of shame, reform themselves."

4. The Master said, "At fifteen I set my heart on learning; at thirty I took my stand; at forty I came to be free from doubts; at fifty I understood the **Decree of Heaven**; at sixty my ear was atuned; at seventy I followed my heart's desire without overstepping the line."

5. **Meng Yi Tzu** asked about being **filial**. The Master answered, "Never fail to comply."

Fan Ch'ih was driving. The Master told him about the interview, saying, "Meng-sun asked me about being filial. I answered, 'Never fail to comply.'"

Fan Ch'ih asked, "What does that mean?"

The Master said, "When your parents are alive, comply with the rites in serving them; when they die, comply with the rites in burying them; comply with the rites in sacrificing to them."

6. Meng Wu Po asked about being filial. The Master said, "Give your father and mother no other cause for anxiety than illness."

7. Tzu-yu asked about being filial. The Master said, "Nowadays for a man to be filial means no more than that he is able to provide his

Decree of Heaven
moral duty as willed by the divine; knowable by the individual who has attained exceptional understanding

Meng Yi Tzu
one among the many of Confucius's students featured in *The Analects*

filial
respectful attitude of children toward parents; a fundamental Confucian virtue

parents with food. Even hounds and horses are, in some way, provided with food. If a man shows no reverence, where is the difference?"

8. Tzu-hsia asked about being filial. The Master said, "What is difficult to manage is the expression on one's face. As for the young taking on the burden when there is work to be done or letting the old enjoy the wine and the food when these are available, that hardly deserves to be called filial."

9. The Master asked, "I can speak to Hui all day without his disagreeing with me in any way. Thus he would seem to be stupid. However, when I take a closer look at what he does in private after he has withdrawn from my presence, I discover that it does, in fact, throw light on what I said. Hui is not stupid after all."

10. The Master said, "Look at the means a man employs, observe the path he takes and examine where he feels at home. In what way is a man's true character hidden from view? In what way is a man's true character hidden from view?"

11. The Master said, "A man is worthy of being a teacher who gets to know what is new by keeping fresh in his mind what he is already familiar with."

gentleman
(Chinese, *chun-tzu*) the mature person who, through diligent learning and practice of virtue, has become an ideal human being with perfect moral character; contrasted with the "small man" (for example, in 2:14)

12. The Master said, "The **gentleman** is no vessel."

13. Tzu-kung asked about the gentleman. The Master said, "He puts his words into action before allowing his words to follow his action."

14. The Master said, "The gentleman enters into associations but not cliques; the small man enters into cliques but not associations."

15. The Master said, "If one learns from others but does not think, one will be bewildered. If, on the other hand, one thinks but does not learn from others, one will be in peril."

16. The Master said, "To attack a task from the wrong end can do nothing but harm."

17. The Master said, "Yu, shall I tell you what it is to know. To say you know when you know, and to say you do not when you do not, that is knowledge."

18. Tzu-chang was studying with an eye to an official career. The Master said, "Use your ears widely but leave out what is doubtful; repeat the rest with caution and you will make few mistakes. Use your eyes widely and leave out what is hazardous; put the rest into practice with caution and you will have few regrets. When in your speech you make few mistakes and in your action you have few regrets, an official career will follow as a matter of course."

19. Duke Ai asked, "What must I do before the common people will look up to me?"

Confucius answered, "Raise the straight and set them over the crooked and the common people will look up to you. Raise the crooked and set them over the straight and the common people will not look up to you."

20. Chi K'ang Tzu asked, "How can one inculcate in the common people the virtue of reverence, of doing their best and of enthusiasm?"

The Master said, "Rule over them with dignity and they will be reverent; treat them with kindness and they will do their best; raise the good and instruct those who are backward and they will be imbued with enthusiasm."

21. Someone said to Confucius, "Why do you not take part in government?"

The Master said, "*The Book of History* says, 'Oh! Simply by being a good son and friendly to his brothers a man can exert an influence upon government.' In so doing a man is, in fact, taking part in government. How can there be any question of his having actively to 'take part in government'?"

22. The Master said, "I do not see how a man can be acceptable who is untrustworthy in word? When a pin is missing in the yoke-bar of a large cart or in the collar-bar of a small cart, how can the cart be expected to go?"

23. Tzu-chang asked, "Can ten generations hence be known?"

The Master said, "The **Yin** built on the rites of the **Hsia**. What was added and what was omitted can be known. The **Chou** built on the rites of the Yin. What was added and what was omitted can be known. Should there be a successor to the Chou, even a hundred generations hence can be known."

Yin . . . Hsia . . . Chou
three dynasties of ancient China; Confucius lived during the Chou (sometimes spelled Zhou) dynasty (1111–249 BC), which was preceded by the Yin (1384–1112 BC), which was preceded centuries before by the Hsia (2183–1752? BC)

24. The Master said, "To offer sacrifice to the spirit of an ancestor not one's own is obsequious.

"Faced with what is right, to leave it undone shows a lack of courage."

Analects on Benevolence

4.2. The Master said, "One who is not benevolent cannot remain long in straitened circumstances, nor can he remain long in easy circumstances.

"The benevolent man is attracted to benevolence because he feels at home in it. The wise man is attracted to benevolence because he finds it to his advantage."

4.3. The Master said, "It is only the benevolent man who is capable of liking or disliking other men."

4.4. The Master said, "If a man sets his heart on benevolence, he will be free from evil."

4.5. The Master said, "Wealth and high station are what men desire but unless I got them in the right way I would not remain in them. Poverty and low station are what men dislike, but even if I did not get these in the right way I would not try to escape from them."

"If the gentleman forsakes benevolence, in what way can he make a name for himself? The gentleman never deserts benevolence, not even for as long as it takes to eat a meal. If he hurries and stumbles one may be sure that it is in benevolence that he does so."

Analects on the Rites

1.12. Yu Tzu said, "Of the things brought about by the rites, harmony is the most valuable. Of the ways of the Former Kings, this is the most beautiful; and is followed alike in matters great and small, yet this will not always work: to aim always at harmony without regulating it by the rites simply because one knows only about harmony will not, in fact, work."

3.3. The Master said, "What can a man do with the rites who is not benevolent? What can a man do with music who is not benevolent?"

12.1 Yen Yüan asked about benevolence. The Master said, "To return to the observance of the rites through overcoming the self constitutes benevolence. If for a single day a man could return to the observance of the rites through overcoming himself, then the whole Empire would consider benevolence to be his. However, the practice of benevolence depends on oneself alone, and not on others."

Yen Yüan said, "I should like you to list the items." The Master said, "Do not look unless it is in accordance with the rites; do not listen unless it is in accordance with the rites; do not speak unless it is in accordance with the rites; do not move unless it is in accordance with the rites."

Yen Yüan said, "Though I am not quick, I shall direct my efforts towards what you have said."

Analects on Learning

7.2. The Master said, "Quietly to store up knowledge in my mind, to learn without flagging, to teach without growing weary, these present me with no difficulties."

7.3. The Master said, "It is these things that cause me concern: failure to cultivate virtue, failure to go more deeply into what I have learned, inability, when I am told what is right, to move to where it is, and inability to reform myself when I have defects."

19.6. Tzu-hsia said, "Learn widely and be steadfast in your purpose, inquire earnestly and reflect on what is at hand, and there is no need for you to look for benevolence elsewhere."

19.7. Tzu-hsia said, "The artisan, in any of the hundred crafts, masters his trade by staying in his workshop; the gentleman perfects his way through learning."

Excerpt from *A Source Book in Chinese Philosophy:* "The Great Learning"

The Way of learning to be great (or adult education) consists in manifesting the clear character, loving the people, and abiding . . . in the highest good.

Only after knowing what to abide in can one be calm. Only after having been calm can one be tranquil. Only after having achieved tranquillity can one have peaceful repose. Only after having peaceful repose can one begin to deliberate. Only after deliberation can the end be attained. Things have their roots and branches. Affairs have their beginnings and their ends. To know what is first and what is last will lead one near the Way.

The ancients who wished to manifest their clear character to the world would first bring order to their states. Those who wished to bring order to their states would first regulate their families.

> **the Way**
> Tao, a fundamental concept in Chinese religious philosophy

investigation of things
In the Confucian tradition, this refers to discerning the most basic reality or principles of things.

Son of Heaven
the emperor

Those who wished to regulate their families would first cultivate their personal lives. Those who wished to cultivate their personal lives would first rectify their minds. Those who wished to rectify their minds would first make their wills sincere. Those who wished to make their wills sincere would first extend their knowledge. The extension of knowledge consists in the **investigation of things.** When things are investigated, knowledge is extended; when knowledge is extended, the will becomes sincere; when the will is sincere, the mind is rectified; when the mind is rectified, the personal life is cultivated; when the personal life is cultivated, the family will be regulated; when the family is regulated, the state will be in order; and when the state is in order, there will be peace throughout the world. From the **Son of Heaven** down to the common people, all must regard cultivation of the personal life as the root or foundation. There is never a case when the root is in disorder and yet the branches are in order. There has never been a case when what is treated with great importance becomes a matter of slight importance or what is treated with slight importance becomes a matter of great importance.

Excerpt from *Confucius: The Secular as Sacred*

by Herbert Fingarette

Consider the sacrificial vessel: in the **original text** Confucius merely names a certain type of jade sacrificial vessel used for holding grain in connection with ceremonies for a bounteous harvest. Such a vessel is holy, sacred. Its outer appearance—the bronze, the carving, the jade—is elegant. Its content, the rich grain, expresses abundance.

Yet the vessel's sacredness does not reside in the preciousness of its bronze, in the beauty of its ornamentation, in the rarity of its jade or in the edibility of the grain. Whence does its sacredness come? It is sacred not because it is useful or handsome but because it is a constitutive element in the ceremony. It is sacred by virtue of its participation in rite, in holy ceremony. In isolation from its role in the ceremony, the vessel is merely an expensive pot filled with grain.

It is therefore a paradox as utensil, for unlike utensils in general, this has no (utilitarian) use external to ceremony itself but only a ritual function.

original text
Fingarette here refers to *The Analects 5:4*, which he cites on a previous page of his book:

Tzu-Kung asked: "What would you say about me as a person?"

The Master said: "You are a utensil."

"What sort of utensil?"

"A sacrificial vase of jade."

(Indeed some ceremonial pots had holes in them in order to emphasize their ritual rather than utilitarian value.)

By analogy, Confucius may be taken to imply that the individual human being, too, has ultimate dignity, sacred dignity by virtue of his role in rite, in ceremony, in *li*. We must recall that Confucius expanded the sense of the word *li*, originally referring to religious ceremonial, in such a way as to envision society itself on the model of *li*. If the teaching about *li* is thus generalized, it is reasonable to follow through and generalize the analogy between Tzu-Kung and the ceremonial vessel. We will then see how this image deepens our understanding of Confucius's teaching about man and human relations.

Social etiquette in general, the father-son relation, the brother-brother relation, the prince-subject relation, the friend-friend relation and the husband-wife relation— persons and their relationships are to be seen as ultimately sanctified by virtue of their place in *li*. Society, at least insofar as regulated by human convention and moral obliga- tions, becomes in the Confucian vision one great ceremonial performance, a ceremony with all the holy beauty of an elaborate religious ritual carried out with that combination of solemnity and lightness of heart that graces the inspired ritual performance. It is not individual existence *per se*, nor is it the existence of a group *per se* that is the condition suf- ficient to create and sustain the ultimate dignity of man. It is the ceremonial aspect of life that bestows sacredness upon persons, acts, and objects which have a role in the perfor- mance of ceremony.

Confucius does not see the individual as an ultimate atom nor society on the analogy of animal or mechanism, nor does he see society as a proving ground for immortal souls or a contractual or utilitarian arrangement designed to maximize individual pleasure. He does not talk in the *Analects* of society and the individual. He talks of what it is to be man, and he sees that man is a special being with a unique dignity and power deriving from and embedded in *li*.

Is it enough merely to be born, to eat, breathe, drink, excrete, enjoy sensual gratification and avoid physical pain and discomfort? Animals do this. To become civilized is to establish relationships that are not merely physical, biological or instinctive; it is to establish *human* relationships, relationships of an essentially symbolic kind, defined by tradition and convention and rooted in respect and obligation.

"Merely to feed one's parents well" . . . "even dogs and horses are fed." (*The Analects* 2:7) To be devoted to one's parents is far more than to keep the parents alive physically. To serve and eat in the proper way, with the proper respect and appreciation, in the proper setting—this is to transform the act of mere nourishment into the human ceremony of dining. To obey the whip is to be not much more than a domestic animal; but to be loyal and faithful to those who rightly govern, to serve them and thus to serve *in* the human community, to do this out of one's own heart and nature—this is to be a true citizen of one's community.

Man's dignity, as does the dignity of things, lies in the ceremony rather than in individual biological existence, and this is evident in the fact that we understand a man who sacrifices his biological existence, his "life" in the biological but not the spiritual sense, if the "rite" demands it. Confucius makes the point succinctly when he responds to his disciple's concern over killing a sheep as an element in a sacrificial rite: "You love the sheep, but I love the ceremony," says Confucius. (*The Analects* 3:17)

"Virtue does not exist in isolation; there must be neighbors," says Confucius. (*The Analects* 4:25) Man is transformed by participation with others in ceremony which is communal. Until he is so transformed he is not truly man but only potentially so—the new-born infant, the wolf-boy of the forests or the "barbarian." Ceremony is justified when we see how it transforms the barbarian into what we know as man at his best. And, from the opposite direction, man at his best is justified when we see that his best is a life of holy ceremony rather than of appetite and mere animal existence. Whichever standpoint we take, we get a perspective on man and society which illuminates and deepens our vision of man's distinctive nature and dignity. When we see man as participant in communal rite rather than as individualistic ego, he takes on to our eyes a new and holy beauty just as does the sacrificial vessel.

Thus, in the *Analects*, man as individual is not sacred. However, he is not therefore to be thought of as a mere utensil to serve "society." For society is no more an independent entity than is ceremony independent of the participants, the holy vessels, the altar, the incantations. Society is men treating each other as men *(jen)*, or to be more specific, according to the obligations and privileges of *li*, out of the love *(ai)* and loyalty *(chung)* and respect *(shu)* called for by their human relationships to each other. The shapes of human relationships are not imposed on man, not physically inevitable, not an instinct or reflex. They are rites learned and voluntarily participated in. The rite is self justifying. The beings, the gestures, the words are not subordinate to rite, nor is rite subordinate to them. To "be self-disciplined and ever turning to *li*" (*The Analects*12:1) is to be no longer at the mercy of animal needs and demoralizing passion, it is to achieve that freedom in which the human spirit flowers; it is not, as **Waley's translation** may lead one to think, a matter of "submission" but of the triumph of the human spirit.

Confucius's theme, then, is not the "discovery of the individual" or of his ultimate importance. The *mere* individual is a bauble, malleable and breakable, a utensil transformed into the resplendent and holy as it serves in the ceremony of life. But then this does not deny *ultimate* dignity to men and to each man; he is not a meaningless ant serving the greater whole. His participation in divinity is as real and clearly visible as is that of the sacrificial vessel, for it is holy. And unlike the way he appears in the Christian view, man is not holy by virtue of his absolute possession, within himself and independently of other men, of a "piece" of the divine, the immortal soul. Nor is the "flowering" of the individual the central theme; instead it is the flowering of humanity in the ceremonial acts of men.

Although the individual must cultivate himself, just as the temple vessel must be carved and chiseled and polished, this self cultivation is no more *central* to man's dignity, in Confucius's views, than the preparation of the vessel is central. Preparation and training are essential, but it is the ceremony that is central, and *all* the elements and

Waley's translation
Arthur Waley's popular translation of *The Analects;* the excerpts featured in this book are from the translation by D. C. Lau

relationships and actions in it are sacred though each has its special characteristics.

Nor should we suppose that Nature is cast out unless shaped into artifact for ritual use. The raiment of holiness is cast upon Nature as well as man, upon the river and the air as well as upon youth and song, when these are seen through the image of a ceremonial Rain Dance. (*The Analects* 11:25)

> **noble man**
>
> the *chun-tzu*, "gentleman," in Lau's translation of *The Analects*

The **noble man** is the man who most perfectly having given up self, ego, obstinacy and personal pride (*The Analects* 9:4) follows not profit but the Way. Such a man has come to fruition as a person; he is the consummate Man. He is a Holy Vessel.

For Reflection

1. Drawing especially from Book II of *The Analects*, describe Confucius's teachings on the good ruler and good government.

2. The fifth of the Ten Commandments, found in the Bible, states: "Honor your father and your mother, so that your days may be long in the land that the LORD your God is giving you" (Exodus 20:12). What similarities and differences do you see between this commandment and Confucius's teachings on being filial?

3. Consider *The Analects 2:17* on knowledge. Interpret in your own words Confucius's teaching. To what extent is this approach to knowledge encouraged in modern society?

4. "The Great Learning" asserts the following in its concluding section: "There is never a case when the root is in disorder and yet the branches are in order." What does this metaphor mean? To what extent do you agree with this teaching?

5. In *Confucius: The Secular as Sacred,* Herbert Fingarette elaborates on Confucius's comparison of a person to a "jade sacrificial vessel." Explain this comparison, showing how the metaphor refers to the person not only as an individual but also as a member of society.

Chapter 7

Taoism

Chinese religion is made up in large part of the complementary traditions of Confucianism and Taoism. Confucian emphasis on learning and the active pursuit of virtue finds its counterpart in Taoist emphasis on naturalness and yielding. Specifically, Taoism teaches the wisdom of yielding to the Tao, the Way of nature. This is embodied in Taoism's primary virtue, *wu-wei*, "actionless activity," letting oneself settle into perfect harmony with nature so nature's energy can empower.

The two founding figures of Taoism are Lao Tzu and Chuang Tzu. Lao Tzu, or "old master" as his name translates, is traditionally thought to be an older contemporary of Confucius (551–479 BC)—if indeed there ever was an actual Lao Tzu. Chuang Tzu is thought to have lived some two hundred years later. The books attributed to them, the *Tao Te Ching* (sometimes simply called the *Lao Tzu*) and the *Chuang Tzu*, have enormously affected East Asian culture for more than two millennia. Our excerpts begin with nineteen chapters of the *Tao Te Ching* (there are eighty-one altogether). Note the paradoxical nature of many of its teachings, as if Lao Tzu was intending to invoke mystery and to prevent the reader from learning in a straightforward manner. The

Tao Te Ching does indeed refute the Confucian insistence on the need for learning. It is for the reader to determine what is to take its place. Note also the various ways by which the text emphasizes *wu-wei*, choosing not to act in order to accomplish something.

The excerpts from the *Chuang Tzu* further exemplify Taoism's paradoxical approach. The observant reader will identify many ways in which these teachings agree with those of the *Tao Te Ching*, although due to its story form, the *Chuang Tzu* tends to present ideas differently. Chuang Tzu at one point tells of having dreamed that he, Chuang Chou (he uses his family name here) was a butterfly. A later story tells of his reaction to his wife's death. Inevitably, these stories challenge the reader to see reality with a wider angle of vision.

Kristofer Schipper's *The Taoist Body* begins with a helpful statement about Taoism as a religion, not only as a philosophy. Taoist philosophy is well known outside China, thanks in large part to the *Chuang Tzu* and the *Tao Te Ching* (of which there are today more than eighty English translations!). In China, Taoism involves much more than these texts, which nonetheless are greatly revered and provide the basis of Taoist religious doctrine. Schipper points out that there are more than one thousand Taoist texts. Taoism has through the centuries also featured many other typically religious aspects, such as priests. Schipper explains that the Taoist priests, or "masters," who have quietly exerted such great influence over the religious culture of China, are becoming scarce. Time will tell if Taoist religion is to maintain a place within China's rapidly changing cultural landscape.

Excerpts from *The Way of Lao Tzu (Tao Te Ching)*

translated by Wing-tsit Chan

1

The Tao that can be told of is not the **eternal Tao;**
The name that can be named is not the eternal name.
The **Nameless** is the origin of Heaven and Earth;
The **Named** is the mother of all things.

Therefore let there always be non-being, so we may
    see their subtlety
And let there always be being, so we may see their outcome.
The two are the same,
But after they are produced, they have different names
They both may be called deep and profound.
Deeper and more profound.
The door of all subtleties!

eternal Tao . . .
Nameless . . .
Named
The opening passage of the *Tao Te Ching* is one of the most cited Chinese passages of all time and admits to no certain interpretation.

2

When the people of the world
all know beauty as beauty,
There arises the recognition of
    ugliness.
When they all know the good
    as good,
There arises the recognition of
    evil.

Therefore:

> Being and non-being produce each other;
> Difficult and easy complete each other;
> Long and short contrast each other;
> High and low distinguish each other;
> Sound and voice harmonize each other;
> Front and behind accompany each other.

Therefore the **sage** manages affairs without action
And spreads doctrines without words.
All things arise, and he does not turn away from them.
He produces them but does not take possession of them.
He acts but does not rely on his own ability.
He accomplishes his task but does not claim credit for it.
It is precisely because he does not claim credit that his
　　accomplishment remains with him.

3

Do not exalt the worthy, so
　　that the people shall not
　　compete.
Do not value rare treasures, so
　　that the people shall not
　　steal.
Do not display objects of de
　　sire, so that the people's
　　heartsshall not be disturbed.

sage
a Taoist master who has distinguished himself through advanced stages of understanding and virtue

Therefore in the government of the sage,
　　He keeps their hearts vacuous,

Fills their bellies,
Weakens their ambitions,
And strengthens their bones,
He always causes his people to be without knowledge
(cunning) or desire,
And the crafty to be afraid to act.
By acting without action, all things will be in order.

8

The best (man) is like water.
Water is good; it benefits all things and does not
compete with them.
It dwells in (lowly) places that all disdain.
This is why it is so near to Tao.

(The best man) in his dwelling loves the earth.
In his heart, he loves what is profound.
In his associations, he loves humanity.
In his words, he loves faithfulness.
In government, he loves order.
In handling affairs, he loves competence.
In his activities, he loves timeliness.
It is because he does not compete that he is
without reproach.

9

To hold and fill a cup to overflowing
Is not as good as to stop in time.
Sharpen a sword-edge to its very sharpest,
And the (edge) will not last long.
When gold and jade fill your hall,

You will not be able to
keep them.
To be proud with honor and
wealth
Is to cause one's own
downfall.
Withdraw as soon as your
work is done.
Such is **Heaven's Way.**

17

The best (rulers) are those whose existence is (merely)
known by the people.
The next best are those who are loved and praised.
The next are those who are feared.
And the next are those who are despised.
It is only when one does not have enough faith in others
that others will have no faith in him.
(The great rulers) value their words highly.
They accomplish their task; they complete their work.
Nevertheless their people say that they simply follow Nature.

22

To yield is to be preserved whole.
To be bent is to become straight.
To be empty is to be full.
To be worn out is to be renewed.
To have little is to possess.
To have plenty is to be perplexed.
Therefore the sage embraces **the One**
And becomes the model of the world.

the One

the original, pure force or reality from which all else has emerged; sometimes identified with Tao

He does not show himself;
   therefore he is luminous.
He does not justify himself;
   therefore he becomes
   prominent.
He does not boast of himself;
   therefore he is given credit.
He does not brag; therefore he can endure for long.

It is precisely because he does not compete that the
   world cannot compete with him.
Is the ancient saying, "To yield is to be preserved whole,"
   empty words?
Truly he will be preserved and (prominence and credit)
   will come to him.

34

The great Tao flows everywhere.
It may go left or right.
All things depend on it for life, and it does
   not turn away from them
It accomplishes its task, but does not claim
   credit for it.
It clothes and feeds all things but does not claim
   to be master over them.

The Small . . . The Great

a typical Taoist juxtaposition of opposites

Always without desires it may
   be called **The Small**.
All things come to it and it
   does not master them;
it may be called **The Great**.
Therefore (the sage) never

strives himself for the
    great, and thereby the great is achieved.

41
When the highest type of men hear Tao,
    They diligently practice it.
When the average type of men hear Tao,
    They half believe in it.
When the lowest type of men hear Tao,
    They laugh heartily at it.
If they did not laugh at it, it would not be Tao.

Therefore there is the established saying:
The Tao which is bright appears to be dark.
The Tao which goes forward appears to fall backward.
The Tao which is level appears uneven.
Great virtue appears like a valley (hollow).
Great purity appears like disgrace.
Far-reaching virtue appears as if insufficient.
Solid virtue appears as if unsteady.
True substance appears to be changeable. The great square
    has no corners.
The great implement (or talent) is slow to finish (or mature).
Great music sounds faint.
Great form has no shape.
Tao is hidden and nameless.
Yet it is Tao alone that skillfully provides for all and brings
    them to perfection.

43

The softest things in the world overcome the hardest
    things in the world.
Non-being penetrates that in which there is no space.
Through this I know the advantage of taking no action.
Few in the world can understand the teaching without words
    and the advantage of taking no actions

47

One may know the world without going out of doors.
One may see the Way of Heaven without looking through
    the windows.
The further one goes, the less one knows.
Therefore the sage knows without going about,
Understands without seeing,
And accomplishes without any action.

48

The pursuit of learning is to increase day after day.
The pursuit of Tao is to decrease day after day.
It is to decrease and further decrease until one reaches the
    point of taking no action.
No action is undertaken, and yet nothing is left undone.
An empire is often brought to order by having no activity.
If one (likes to) undertake activity, he is not qualified to
    govern the empire.

49

The sage has no fixed (personal) ideas.
He regards the people's ideas as his own.
I treat those who are good with goodness,

And I also treat those who are not good with goodness.
Thus goodness is attained.
I am honest to those who are honest,
And I am also honest to those who are not honest.
Thus honesty is attained.
The sage, in the government of his empire, has no subjective
    viewpoint.
His mind forms a harmonious whole with that of his people.
They all lend their eyes and ears, and he treats them all
    as infants.

56
He who knows does not speak.
He who speaks does not know.

Close the mouth.
Shut the doors.
Blunt the sharpness.
Untie the tangles.
Soften the light.
Become one with the dusty worlds.
This is called profound identification.

Therefore it is impossible either to be intimate and
    close to him or to be distant and indifferent to him.
It is impossible either to benefit him or to harm him.
It is impossible either to honor him or to disgrace him.
For this reason he is honored by the world.

63

Act without action.

Do without ado.

Taste without tasting.

Whether it is big or small, many or few, repay
hatred with virtue.

Prepare for the difficult while it is still easy.

Deal with the big while it is still small.

Difficult undertakings have always started with what
is easy.

And great undertakings have always started with what
is small.

Therefore the sage never strives for the great,

And thereby the great is achieved.

He who makes rash promises surely lacks faith.

He who takes things too easily will surely encounter
much difficulty.

For this reason even the sage regards things as difficult.

And therefore he encounters no difficulty.

70

My doctrines are very easy to understand and very easy to
practice,

But none in the world can understand or practice them.

My doctrines have a source (Nature); my deeds have a
master (Tao).

It is because people do not understand this that they do not
understand me.

Few people know me, and therefore I am highly valued.

Therefore the sage wears a coarse cloth on top and carries
jade within his bosom.

71

To know that you do not know is the best.

To pretend to know when you do not know is a disease.

Only when one recognizes this disease as a disease can one
be free from the disease.

The sage is free from the disease.

Because he recognizes this disease to be disease, he is free
from it.

78

There is nothing softer and weaker than water,

And yet there is nothing better for attacking hard and
strong things.

For this reason there is no substitute for it,

All the world knows that the weak overcomes the strong and
the soft overcomes the hard.

But none can practice it.

Therefore the sage says:

He who suffers disgrace for his country
Is called the lord of the land.
He who takes upon himself the country's misfortunes
Becomes the king of the empire.

Straight words seem to be their opposite.

81

True words are not beautiful;
Beautiful words are not true.
A good man does not argue;
He who argues is not a good man.
A wise man has no extensive knowledge;
He who has extensive knowledge is not a wise man.

The sage does not accumulate for himself.
The more he uses for others, the more he has himself.
The more he gives to others, the more he possesses
    of his own.
The Way of Heaven is to benefit others and not to injure.
The Way of the sage is to act but not to compete.

(Used with permission of Pearson Education, Upper Saddle River,
New Jersey.)

Excerpts from *Chuang Tzu: Basic Writings*

translated by Burton Watson

to the spirits and to God
There is little mention of God or other supernatural beings in the *Chuang Tzu* (the Chinese term here can also be translated as "ruler"); the mention here of "spirits" and "God" should not be taken as being highly significant for the overall perspective of the book.

The Way has its reality and its signs but is without action or form. You can hand it down but you cannot receive it; you can get it but you cannot see it. It is its own source, its own root. Before Heaven and earth existed it was there, firm from ancient times. It gave spirituality **to the spirits and to God;** it gave birth to Heaven and to earth. It exists beyond the highest point, and yet you cannot call it lofty; it exists beneath the limit of the six directions, and yet you cannot call it deep. It was born before Heaven and earth, and yet you cannot say it has been there for long; it is earlier than the earliest time, and yet you cannot call it old. . . .

Nan-po Tzu k'uei said to the Woman Crookback, "You are old in years and yet your complexion is that of a child. Why is this?"

"I have heard the Way!"

"Can the Way be learned?" asked Nan-po Tzu-k'uei.

"Goodness, how could that be? Anyway, you aren't the man to do it. Now there's **Pu-liang Yi**—he has the talent of a sage but not the Way of a sage, whereas I have the Way of a sage but not the talent of a sage. I thought I would try to teach him and see if I could really get anywhere near to making him a sage. It's easier to explain the Way of a sage to someone who has the talent of a sage, you know. So I began explaining and kept at him for three days, and after that he was able to put the world outside himself. When he had put the world outside himself, I kept at him for seven days more, and after that he was able to put things outside himself. When he had put things outside himself, I kept at him for nine days more, and after that he was able to put life outside himself. After he had put life outside himself, he was able to achieve the brightness of dawn, and when he had achieved the brightness of dawn, he could see his

> **Nan-po Tzu k'uei . . . Pu-liang Yi**
> The *Chuang Tzu* is filled with anecdotes involving various characters, some historical, some not; we need not concern ourselves with the details of these two.

own aloneness. After he had managed to see his own alone-ness, he could do away with past and present, and after he had done away with past and present, he was able to enter where there is no life and no death. That which kills life does not die; that which gives life to life does not live. This is the kind of thing it is: there's nothing it doesn't send off, noth-ing it doesn't welcome, nothing it doesn't destroy, nothing it doesn't complete. Its name is Peace-in-Strife. After the strife, it attains completion." . . .

Once **Chuang Chou** dreamt he was a butterfly, a but-terfly flitting and fluttering around, happy with himself and doing as he pleased. He didn't know he was Chuang Chou. Suddenly he woke up and there he was, solid and unmistak-able Chuang Chou. But he didn't know if he was Chuang Chou who had dreamt he was a butterfly, or a butterfly dreaming he was Chuang Chou. Between Chuang Chou and a butterfly there must be *some* distinction! This is called the Transformation of Things. . . .

"What's more, we go around telling each other, I do this, I do that—but how do we know that this 'I' we talk about has any 'I' to it? You dream you're a bird and soar up into the sky; you dream you're a fish and dive down in the pool. But now when you tell me about it, I don't know whether you are awake or whether you are dreaming. Running around accus-ing others is not as good as laughing, and enjoying a good laugh is not as good as going along with things. Be content to go along and forget about change and then you can enter the mysterious oneness of Heaven." . . .

Chuang Chou
as noted in the introduc-tion, this is Chuang Tzu, here using his family name.

Chuang Tzu's wife died. When **Hui Tzu** went to convey his condolences, he found Chuang Tzu sitting with his legs sprawled out, pounding on a tub and singing. "You lived with her, she brought up your

Hui Tzu
(family name Hui Shih)
a notable philosopher
of logic and apparently
Chuang Tzu's friend

children and grew old," said Hui Tzu. "It should be enough simply not to weep at her death. But pounding on a tub and singing—this is going too far, isn't it?"

Chuang Tzu said, "You're wrong. When she first died, do you think I didn't grieve like anyone else? But I looked back to her beginning and the time before she was born. Not only the time before she was born, but the time before she had a body. Not only the time before she had a body, but the time before she had a spirit. In the midst of the jumble of wonder and mystery a change took place and she had a spirit. Another change and she had a body. Another change and she was born. Now there's been another change and she's dead. It's just like the progression of the four seasons, spring, summer, fall, winter.

"Now she's going to lie down peacefully in a vast room. If I were to follow after her bawling and sobbing, it would show that I don't understand anything about fate. So I stopped."

Excerpt from *The Taoist Body*

by Kristofer Schipper

Chuang Tzu tells about a conversation among four Taoists:

Who can think of nothingness as his head, of life as his spine, of death as his buttocks! Who knows that life and death, consciousness and unconsciousness are all one body? He shall be my friend! The four looked at each other and laughed. They felt no opposition and thus they became friends.

A little further on, the same book tells us about three other friends who talk among themselves:

Who can join with others without "joining with others?" Who can do something with others, without "doing something with others?" Who can go up to heaven [make himself one with nature], wander in the mists [of mystery], dance in the Infinite, become oblivious of life, forever, without end? The three looked at each other and laughed. They felt no opposition in their hearts and thus they became friends.

These texts come from the oldest part of the book of the philosopher Chuang Tzu (the *Chuang-tzu*), itself one of the most ancient Taoist texts which has come down to us. They tell us about a certain relationship between the physical body, the cosmic body, and the social body, that of the "friends in the Tao." Even today, Taoist masters call each other "friends" when they address one another. Never very numerous, these priests of the true religious and philosophical traditions of China are nowadays few indeed. As to their traditions, they are comparable, to a certain degree to the ancient mystery religions of Greece and the Hellenistic world, which vanished at the end of the age of Antiquity. Today, Taoism is threatened with a similar fate, and its disappearance, which may be near at hand, will leave our knowledge of the religion of ancient China quite incomplete.

Not that great efforts have been made to understand China's religion up to now! In the course of its history, China has known and assimilated all the major creeds of the world: Buddhism, Islam, Judaism, Christianity, and even Hinduism, which was introduced through the intermediary of **Tantric Buddhism.** All these religions have had their moment of glory, have been in fashion for longer or shorter periods, before being slowly absorbed into the **Middle Kingdom,** which integrated them into its own culture, though not without first introducing profound modifications. In scholarly works these religions of foreign origin occupy a prominent position. There are, for instance, countless studies on the history of Buddhism or the history of the Jesuits in China. In contrast, very little is made of the religion that preceded them and that has survived them all: Taoism, the religion of the Chinese themselves. And yet, to understand the history and

Tantric Buddhism
Vajrayana Buddhism, the prominent form among the Tibetans

Middle Kingdom
China

the fate of the other beliefs, one must always refer to Taoism; for it was mainly under its influence, direct or indirect, that the foreign creeds were transformed. To cite one famous example, Indian Buddhism was changed into that radically different form of Chinese Buddhism called *ch'an* (better known under its Japanese name of Zen).

The Notion of Religion

The widespread ignorance concerning Taoism can by no means be imputed to the nature of Chinese religion as such: until the persecutions that descended on it a century ago and which still go on, it was alive, visible, and accessible in daily life. Taoism moreover, which can be seen as the most elevated expression of Chinese popular religion, possesses a rich and vast literature, comprising more than a thousand works, covering all aspects of its traditions. Rather, this loss of interest on the part of western scholars is due, I think, to the difficulty in understanding Chinese religion. The very notion of religion as we define it in the west is an obstacle, and a great number of observers have fallen into the trap of failing to see that in a society so dissimilar from ours the religious system must also be very different.

In everyday life, religious activity had no particular name or status, since—as the French **sinologist** Marcel Granet was fond of pointing out—in China, religion was formerly not distinguished from social activity in general. Even its most distinguished representatives, the Taoist masters, were generally integrated in

sinologist
a specialist in Chinese culture

lay society and enjoyed no special status. In modern times and in imitation of Western culture and its concept of religion as something setting humanity apart from nature, the authorities have applied themselves to the task of classifying and dividing the people, trying in vain to convince the ordinary peasant that he was either a Confucian, a Buddhist, a Taoist, or, more recently still—in keeping with the party line—simply "superstitious." In fact, none of this really applies and certainly no ordinary person would call himself a Taoist, since this designation always implies an initiation into the Mysteries, and consequently is even now reserved for the masters, the local sages.

Traditionally, no special term existed to express religious activity. In order to translate our word *religion*, modern Chinese usage has coined the term *tsung-chiao*, literally "sectarian doctrine." This may be correct for Islam or Catholicism, but when this term is used for the Chinese popular religion and its highest expression, Taoism—that is to say, a religion which considers itself to be the true bond among all beings without any doctrinal creed, profession of faith, or dogmatism—it can only create misunderstandings.

For Reflection

1. "If [the lowest type of men] did not laugh at it, it would not be Tao" (*Tao Te Ching*, chapter 41). Explain the meaning of this passage.

2. Consider the teachings of the *Tao Te Ching*, chapter 49, on how to treat others. Compare these teachings with the statements of Jesus in the Sermon on the Mount, specifically in Matthew 5:43–48 (found in chapter 10 of this book).

3. The *Tao Te Ching* and the *Chuang Tzu* include many paradoxical statements—assertions that seem illogical and contradictory but are intended to reveal deeper truths. Identify at least two paradoxical statements in the texts and offer your interpretations of their intended meaning.

4. Drawing on the story of his wife's death, explain Chuang Tzu's perspective on death. To what extent does it seem compatible with other Taoist teachings?

5. Kristofer Schipper cites as an obstacle to "understanding Chinese religion" the "very notion of religion as we define it in the west . . ." Based on what you have learned about Taoism (and perhaps other Chinese religions such as Confucianism and Buddhism), identify some aspects of the Christian notion of religion that Schipper might have in mind.

Chapter 8

Shinto

Shinto is the traditional religion of Japan. Like the cultures of
China and other East Asian lands, Japanese culture incorporates other traditions: most notably, Buddhism, Confucianism, and Taoism. Shinto emphasizes the Japanese mythic
understanding of the origins of the Japanese islands, their
inhabitants, and their natural wonders. All these things are
celebrated through worship of the *kami*, a broad category
that includes anything the Japanese hold as sacred. Shinto
also emphasizes ritual and incorporates a wide array of
means of worshiping the *kami*. The traditional Japanese
home contains a *kamidana*, or "*kami* shelf." Worship of the
kami outdoors features the torii, the pillared archways that
mark the entrances to Shinto shrines and that symbolize the
tradition. Many of Japan's festivals also feature ritual worship
of the *kami*. The various forms of Shinto worship emphasize
ritual purity. To be in the presence of the *kami*, one ought to
embody the original purity of nature.

Along with its emphasis on ritual, Shinto features myth.
In this chapter we cite ancient renditions of the most important foundational myths of Japan. Several features of myth,
highlighted in chapter 2, are exhibited in Shinto myths: they
answer fundamental questions and provide explanations to
basic human concerns, they are typically set in primordial

time, and they commonly are populated by supernatural beings. The first two excerpts are drawn from the *Nihongi* and the *Kijoki*, two ancient collections of Shinto myth. The first myth recounts the birth of Amaterasu, the Sun Goddess, one of several offspring of the primal divine couple, Izanagi and Izanami. The second recounts the creation of the divine imperial ancestors. Eventually, according to further accounts, this line of descent would produce Japan's first human emperor, and he in turn would be the ancestor of a line of imperial descendants that has lasted to the present day. Taken together through the centuries, these two myths provide the Japanese people with justification for the authority they have invested in their emperor, the direct descendant of Izanagi and Izanami. This primal pair also was responsible for creating the islands that make up Japan. Shinto myth thus provides for the people a powerful bond between the land and the society.

Motoori Norinaga (1730–1801) is regarded as one of Shinto's greatest scholars. In "The True Tradition of the Sun Goddess," Norinaga makes clear his belief in the inherent superiority of Japan. Confirming the accounts as recorded in the *Nihongi* and the *Kijoki*, Norinaga refers to the special regard of the Sun Goddess, "the forbear of the nation," for Japan.

In our last excerpt, Norinaga sets forth his famous statement on the *kami*. Remarkably, even a scholar of his standing must admit that he does "not yet understand the meaning of the term, *kami*." Norinaga nevertheless goes on to provide the most authoritative description of the *kami* ever to have been written.

Excerpts from *Sources of Japanese Tradition:* Shinto Creation Myth

Birth of the Sun Goddess

Izanagi no Mikoto and Izanami no Mikoto consulted together, saying: "We have now produced the **Great-eight-island country,** with the mountains, rivers, herbs, and trees. Why should we not produce someone who shall be lord of the universe?" They then together produced the Sun Goddess, who was called Ō-hiru-me no muchi.

(Called in one writing Amaterasu no Ō kami.)

(In one writing she is called Amaterasu-Ō -hiru-me no Mikoto.)

The resplendent luster of this child shone throughout all the **six quarters.** Therefore the two Deities rejoiced, saying: "We have had many children, but none of them have been equal to this wondrous infant. She ought not to be kept long in this land, but we ought of our own accord to send her at once to Heaven, and entrust to her the affairs of Heaven."

At this time Heaven and Earth were still not far separated, and therefore they sent her up to Heaven by the ladder of Heaven.

They next produced the Moon-god.

Great-eight-island country
Japan

six quarters
the four directions, along with above and below

(Called in one writing Tsuki-yumi no Mikoto, or Tsuki-yomi no Mikoto.)

His radiance was next to that of the Sun in splendor. This God was to be the consort of the Sun Goddess, and to share in her government. They therefore sent him also to Heaven.

Next they produced the leech-child, which even at the age of three years could not stand upright. They therefore placed it in the rock-camphor-wood boat of Heaven, and abandoned it to the winds.

Their next child was Sosa no o no Mikoto.

(Called in one writing Kami Sosa-no-o no Mikoto or Haya Sosa-no-o no Mikoto.)

This God had a fierce temper and was given to cruel acts. Moreover he made a practice of continually weeping and wailing. So he brought many of the people of the land to an untimely end. Again he caused green mountains to become withered. Therefore the two Gods, his parents, addressed Sosa no o no Mikoto, saying: "Thou art exceedingly wicked, and it is not meet that thou shouldst reign over the world. Certainly thou must depart far away to the Netherland." So they at length expelled him.

The Divine Creation of the Imperial Ancestors

So thereupon His-Swift-Impetuous-Male-Augustness (**Susano-o**) said: "If that be so, I will take leave of the Heaven-Shining-Great-August-Deity (Amaterasu), and depart." [With these words] he forthwith went up to Heaven, whereupon all the mountains and rivers shook, and every land and country quaked. So the Heaven-Shining-Deity, alarmed at the noise, said: "The reason of the ascent hither of His Augustness my elder brother is surely no good intent. It is only that he wishes to wrest my land from me." And she forthwith, unbinding her august hair, twisted it into august bunches; and both into the left and into the right august bunch, as likewise into

her august head-dress and likewise on to her left and her right august arm, she twisted an augustly complete [string] of curved jewels eight feet [long] of five hundred jewels; and, slinging on her back a quiver holding a thousand [arrows], and adding [thereto] a quiver holding five hundred [arrows], she likewise took and slung at her side a mighty and high [-sounding] elbow-pad, and brandished and stuck her bow upright so that the top shook; and she stamped her feet into the hard ground up to her opposing thighs, kicking away [the earth] like rotten snow, and stood valiantly like unto a mighty man, and, waiting, asked: "Wherefore ascended thou hither?"Then Susa-no-o replied, saying : "I have no evil intent. It is only that when the Great-August-Deity [our father] spoke, deigning to enquire the cause of my wailing and weeping, I said: 'I wail because I wish to go to my deceased mother's land'; whereupon the Great-August-Deity said: 'Thou shalt not dwell in this land,' and deigned to expel me with a divine expulsion. It is therefore, solely with the thought of taking leave of thee and departing, that I have ascended hither. I have no strange intentions." Then the Heaven-Shining-Deity said: "If that be so, whereby

> **Deities that were born from the mist [of her breath]**
> Three female divine imperial ancestors, named in the following sentences, are born from Amaterasu's breath.

> **Deity that was born from the mist [of his breath]**
> five male divine imperial ancestors, named in the following sentences, are born from Susa-no-o's breath

shall I know the sincerity of thine intentions?" Thereupon Susa-no-o replied, saying "Let each of us swear, and produce children." So as they then swore to each other from the opposite banks of the Tranquil River of Heaven, the august names of the **Deities that were born from the mist [of her breath]** when, having first begged Susa-no-o to hand her the ten-grasp saber which was girded on him and broken it into three fragments, and with the jewels making a jingling sound having brandished and washed them in the True-Pool-Well of Heaven, and having crunchingly crunched them, the Heaven-Shining-Deity blew them away, were Her August-ness Torrent-Mist-Princess, another august name for whom is Her Augustness Princess-of-the-Island-of-the-Offing; next Her Augustness Lovely-Island-Princess, another august name for whom is Her Augustness Good-Princess; next Her Augustness Princess-of-the-Torrent. The august name of the **Deity that was born from the mist [of his breath]** when, having begged the Heaven-Shining-Deity to hand him the augustly complete [string] of curved jewels eight feet [long] of five hundred jewels that was twisted in the left august bunch [of her hair], and with the jewels making a jingling sound hav-ing brandished and washed them in the True-Pool-Well of

Heaven, and having crunchingly crunched them, Susa-no-o blew them away, was His Augustness Truly-Conqueror-I-Conquer-Conquering-Swift-Heavenly-Great-Great-Ears. The august name of the Deity that was born from the mist [of his breath] when again, having begged her to hand him the jewels that were twisted in the right august bunch [of her hair], and having crunchingly crunched them, he blew them away, was His Augustness Ame-no-hohi. The august name of the Deity that was born from the mist [of his breath] when again, having begged her to hand him the jewels that were twisted in her august head-dress, and having crunchingly crunched them, he blew them away, was His Augustness Prince-Lord-of-Heaven. The august name of the Deity that was born from the mist [of his breath] when again, having begged her to hand him the jewels that were twisted on her left august arm, and having crunchingly crunched them, he blew them away, was His Augustness Prince-Lord-of-Life. The august name of the Deity that was born from the jewels that were twisted on her right august arm, and having crunchingly crunched them, he blew them away, was His-Wondrous-Augustness-of-Kumanu. [Five Deities in all.]

Excerpt from *Motoori Norinaga Zerish:* "The True Tradition of the Sun Goddess"

by Motoori Norinaga

The True Way is one and the same, in every country and throughout heaven and earth. This Way, however, has been

Takami-musubi and Kami-musubi
divine forces of vitality and fertility, respectively

yin and yang
according to Chinese religious philosophy, the complementary components of the universe; yin is passive, feminine, and earthly, whereas yang is active, masculine, and heavenly

hexagrams of the Book of Changes
The *I Ching (Book of Changes)* is a foundational text of Chinese religious philosophy; its primary method of expressing ideas is through a series of hexagrams (six-lined figures of varying configurations)

correctly transmitted only in our Imperial Land. Its transmission in all foreign countries was lost long ago in early antiquity, and many and varied ways have been expounded, each country representing its own way as the Right Way. But the ways of foreign countries are no more the original Right Way than end-branches of a tree are the same as its root. They may have resemblances here and there to the Right Way, but because the original truth has been corrupted with the passage of time, they can scarcely be likened to the original Right Way. Let me state briefly what that one original Way is. One must understand, first of all, the universal principle of the world. The principle is that Heaven and earth, all the gods and all phenomena, were brought into existence by the creative spirits of two deities—**Takami-musubi and Kami-musubi.** The birth of all humankind in all ages and the existence of all things and all matter have been the result of that creative spirit. It was the original creativity of these two august deities which caused the deities Izanagi and Izanami to create the land, all kinds of phenomena, and numerous gods and goddesses at the beginning of the Divine Age. This spirit of creativity [*musubi*, lit., "union"] is a miraculously divine act the reason for which is beyond the comprehension of the human intellect.

But in the foreign countries where the Right Way has not been transmitted this act of divine creativity is not known. Men there have tried to explain the principle of Heaven and earth and all phenomena by such theories as the **yin and yang,** the **hexagrams of the Book of Changes,** and the **Five Elements.** But all of these are fallacious theories stemming from the assumptions of the human intellect and they in no wise represent the true principle.

Izanagi, in deep sorrow at the passing of his goddess, journeyed after her to the land of death. Upon his return to the upper world he bathed himself at **Ahagiwara in Tachibana Bay in Tsukushi** in order to purify himself of the pollution of the land of death, and while thus cleansing himself,

> **Five Elements**
> According to Chinese religious philosophy, the fundamental building blocks of matter are water, fire, wood, metal, and earth.

> **Izanagi, in deep sorrow at the passing of his goddess**
> In a section of the mythic narrative not included in our excerpts, Izanami dies.

> **Ahagiwara in Tachibana Bay in Tsukushi**
> Tachibana Bay is in western Kyushu (ancient name: Tsukushi), one of the main islands of Japan.

he gave birth to the Heaven-Shining Goddess who by the explicit command of her father-God, came to rule the Heavenly Plain for all time to come. This Heaven-Shining Goddess is none other than the sun in heaven which today casts its gracious light over the world. Then, an Imperial Prince of the Heaven-Shining Goddess was sent down from heaven to the middle kingdom of Ashihara. In the Goddess' mandate to the Prince at that time it was stated that his dynasty should be coeval with heaven and earth. It is this mandate which is the very origin and basis of the Way. Thus, all the principles of the world and the way of humankind are represented in the different stages of the Divine Age. Those who seek to know the Right Way must therefore pay careful attention to the stages of the Divine Age and learn the truths of existence. These aspects of the various stages are embodied in the ancient traditions of the Divine Age. No one knows with whom these ancient traditions began, but they were handed down orally from the very earliest times and they refer to the accounts which have since been recorded in the *Kijoki* and the *Nihongi*. The accounts recorded in these two scriptures are clear and explicit and present no cause for doubt. Those who have interpreted these scriptures in a later age have contrived oracular formulae and have expounded theories which have no real basis. Some have become addicts of foreign doctrines and have no faith in the wonders of the Divine Age. Unable to understand that the truths of the world are contained in the evolution of the Divine Age, they fail to ascertain the true meaning of our ancient tradition. As they base their judgment on the strength of foreign belief they always interpret at their own discretion and twist to their own liking anything they encounter which may not be in accord with their alien teachings. Thus, they say that the High Heavenly Plain refers to the Imperial Capital and not to Heaven, and that the Sun Goddess herself was not a goddess nor the sun shining in the heavens but an earthly person and the forebear of the nation. These are arbitrary interpretations purposely contrived to flatter foreign ideologies. In this way the ancient tradition is made to appear narrow and petty, by depriving it of its comprehensive and primal character. This is counter to the meaning of the scriptures.

Heaven and earth are one; there is no barrier between them. The High Heavenly Plain is the high heavenly plain which covers all the countries of the world, and the Sun Goddess is the goddess who reigns in that heaven. Thus, she is without a peer in the whole universe, casting her light to the very ends of heaven and earth and for all time. There is not a single country in the world which does not receive her beneficent illuminations, and no country can exist even for a day or an hour bereft of her grace. This goddess is the splendor of all splendors. However, foreign countries, having lost the ancient tradition of the Divine Age, do not know the meaning of revering this goddess. Only through the speculations of the human intelligence have they come to call the sun and the moon the spirit of yang and yin. In China and other countries the "Heavenly Emperor" is worshiped as the supreme divinity. In other countries there are other objects of reverence, each according to its own way, but their teachings are based, some on the logic of inference, and some on arbitrary personal opinions. At any rate, they are merely man-made designations and the "Heavenly Ruler" or the "Heavenly Way" have no real existence at all. That foreign countries revere such nonexistent beings and remain unaware of the grace of the Sun Goddess is a matter of profound regret. However, because of the special dispensation of our Imperial Land, the ancient tradition of the Divine Age has been correctly and clearly transmitted in our country, telling us of the genesis of the great goddess and the reason for her adoration. The "special dispensation of our Imperial Land" means that ours is the native land of the Heaven-Shining Goddess who casts her light over all countries in the four seas. Thus our country is the source and fountainhead of all other countries, and in all matters it excels all the others. It would be impossible to list all the products in which our country excels, but foremost among them is rice, which sustains the life of man, for whom there is no product more important. Our country's rice has no peer in foreign countries, from which fact it may be seen why our other products are also superior. Those who were born in this country have long been accustomed to our rice and take it for granted, unaware of its excellence. They enjoy such excellent rice morning and night to their heart's content because they have been fortunate enough to be born in this country. This is a matter for which they should give thanks to our shining deities, but to my great dismay they seem to be unmindful of it.

Our country's Imperial Line, which casts its light over this world, represents the descendants of the Sky-Shining Goddess. And in accordance with that Goddess' mandate of reigning "forever and ever, coeval with Heaven and earth," the Imperial Line is destined to rule the nation for eons until the end of time and as long as the universe exists. That is the very basis of our Way. That our history has not deviated from the instructions of the divine mandate bears testimony to the infallibility of our ancient tradition. It can also be seen why foreign countries cannot match ours and what is meant by the special dispensation of our country. Foreign countries expound their own ways, each as if its way alone were true. But their dynastic lines, basic to their existence, do not continue, they change frequently and are quite corrupt. Thus one can surmise that in everything they say there are falsehoods and that there is no basis in fact for them.

"The Meaning of *Kami*"

by Motoori Norinaga

"I do not yet understand the meaning of the term, *kami*. Speaking in general, however, it may be said that *kami* signifies, in the first place, the deities of heaven and earth that appear in the ancient records and also the spirits of the shrines where they are worshipped.

"It is hardly necessary to say that it includes human beings. It also includes such objects as birds, beasts, trees, plants, seas, mountains and so forth. In ancient usage, anything whatsoever which was outside the ordinary, which possessed superior power or which was awe-inspiring was called *kami*. Eminence here does not refer merely to the superiority of nobility, goodness or meritorious deeds. Evil and mysterious things, if they are extraordinary and dreadful, are called *kami*. It is needless to say that among human beings who are called kami the successive generations of sacred emperors are all included. The fact that emperors are also called 'distant *kami*' is because, from the standpoint of common people, they are far-separated, majestic and worthy of reverence. In a lesser degree we find, in the present as well as in ancient times, human beings who are *kami*. Although they may not be accepted throughout the whole country, yet in each province, each village and each family there are human beings who are *kami*, each one according to his own proper position. The *kami* of the divine age were for the most part human beings of that time and, because the people of that time were all *kami*, it is called the Age of the Gods (kami).

"Furthermore, among things which are not human, the thunder is always called 'sounding-*kami*'. Such things as dragons, the echo, and foxes, inasmuch as they are conspicuous, wonderful and awe-inspiring, are also *kami*. In popular usage the echo is said to be **tengu** and in Chinese writings it is referred to as a mountain goblin. . . .

"In the Nihongi and the **Manyōshū** the tiger and the wolf are also spoken of as *kami*. Again there are the cases in which peaches were given the name, August-Thing-Great-Kamu Fruit, and a necklace was called August-Storehouse-shelf-Kami. There are further instances in which rocks, stumps of trees and leaves of plants spoke audibly. They were all *kami*. There are again numerous places in which seas and mountains are called *kami*. This does not have reference to the spirit of the mountain or the sea, but *kami* is used here directly of the particular mountain or sea. This is because they were exceedingly awe-inspiring."

tengu
a winged goblin believed to inhabit forests and mountains

Manyōshū
anthology of Japanese poetry compiled in the eighth century AD

For Reflection

1. Consider the episode of the expulsion of Sosa no o no Mikoto in "Birth of the Sun Goddess." What does this segment of the myth suggest regarding Japanese norms of behavior?

2. In "The True Tradition of the Sun Goddess," Motoori Norinaga uses the analogy of the branches of a tree and its root to compare the "True Way" of Shinto with the varying interpretations of other lands. Mahatma Gandhi in one of his writings also draws on the analogy of a tree to explain the relation of religious traditions (see the excerpt from *Yeravda Mandir* in chapter 3, page 59, of this book). Compare the perspectives of Norinaga and Gandhi on the relation of religions as expressed through this common analogy.

3. Consider Norinaga's "True Tradition of the Sun Goddess." What would a traditional follower of Shinto likely find significant or meaningful in this story?

4. Norinaga refers to his rendition of the myth of the Sun Goddess as the "True Way." What does his claim mean for the Japanese and for the people of other lands?

5. Drawing from Norinaga's description of the *kami*, identify the various categories of *kami*. What do you find surprising or especially notable about the *kami*?

Chapter 9

Judaism

Though numerically a relatively small religion—there are about fourteen million Jews worldwide—Judaism has, from its beginnings, contributed significantly to the world's religious landscape. Judaism was the first major religion to embrace monotheism, a belief in only one God. More precisely, Judaism embraces ethical monotheism—the belief that the only God is perfectly good and is concerned about the moral quality of human lives. Because of the Covenant, an agreement established between God and the ancient Israelites, the Jews understand themselves to be God's Chosen People, with special rights and responsibilities. Like most religions, Judaism contains within it a spectrum of religious perspectives, from the very conservative to the very liberal. The primary sources in this chapter serve to illustrate various aspects of Judaism, beginning with the biblical account of the foundational event of God's giving of the Torah, or Law, at Mount Sinai, found today in Egypt.

The event narrated in the Book of Exodus, chapters 19–20 takes place during the course of the Exodus of the Israelites from Egypt, believed by most biblical scholars to have occurred about 1280 BC. Moses and the Israelite people, having miraculously crossed the Red Sea, arrive at

Mount Sinai, where God speaks to Moses. Before setting forth the Ten Commandments (see Exodus 20:1–17), God establishes with the Israelites the Covenant, according to which the Israelites are to be "a priestly kingdom and a holy nation" (Exodus 19:5–6). Such are the special responsibilities of the Chosen People—they are to maintain a heightened level of righteousness before God.

The religion of Judaism, as it is practiced today, took shape during the classical, or rabbinic, period from the end of the first century AD through the seventh century. It was during this period that the Mishna, the Talmud, and other rabbinic texts were produced. Our second excerpt features one of the sayings from the *Pirke Aboth*, or "sayings of the fathers," which is one of the sixty-three tractates of the Mishna. The saying itself, which focuses on "loving peace" and "loving thy fellow creatures" and is attributed to the famous rabbi Hillel, is set forth at the beginning of the excerpt. Translator Isaac Unterman then proceeds to provide information about Hillel, an important founding figure of rabbinic Judaism. Unterman concludes by setting forth a variety of rabbinic sources relating to this particular saying. Taken in full, the material in this excerpt offers an illuminating glimpse into the world of the rabbinic period.

Allegra Goodman's *Family Markowitz* is a collection of short stories that follow a family over the course of three generations. This chapter's excerpt from the story "The Four Questions" features the family at the Passover seder hosted at the Long Island home of Sol and Estelle. Their twenty-three-year-old daughter, Miriam, a student at Harvard Medical School, has recently become more traditional, or orthodox, in her practice of Judaism, clearly to the frustration of Ed Markowitz, her liberal father. We join the family at the dinner table as they commence the ritual celebration of Passover.

Exodus, Chapters 19–20

Chapter 19

The Israelites Reach Mount Sinai

[1]On the third new moon after the Israelites had gone out of the land of Egypt, on that very day, they came into the wilderness of Sinai. [2]They had journeyed from Rephidim, entered the wilderness of Sinai, and camped in the wilderness; Israel camped there in front of the mountain. [3]Then Moses went up to God; **the Lord** called to him from the mountain, saying, "Thus you shall say to the **house of Jacob,** and tell the Israelites: [4]You have seen what I did to the Egyptians, and how I bore you on eagles' wings and brought you to myself. [5]Now therefore, if you obey my voice and keep my covenant, you shall be my

the Lord
Because the name of God, written in the Bible in the Hebrew equivalents of the letters YHWH, is considered by observant Jews as too holy to pronounce, "the Lord" is often substituted in English translations; in other contexts, the name is commonly spelled and pronounced (though not by observant Jews) as Yahweh.

treasured possession out of all the peoples. Indeed, the whole earth is mine, ⁶but you shall be for me a priestly kingdom and a holy nation. These are the words that you shall speak to the Israelites."

house of Jacob
the Israelites; for the biblical episode in which God gives Jacob the name Israel, see Genesis 32:28

So Moses came, summoned the elders of the people, and set before them all these words that the LORD had commanded him. ⁸The people all answered as one: "Everything that the LORD has spoken we will do." Moses reported the words of the people to the LORD. ⁹Then the LORD said to Moses, "I am going to come to you in a dense cloud, in order that the people may hear when I speak with you and so trust you ever after."

The People Consecrated

When Moses had told the words of the people to the LORD, ¹⁰the LORD said to Moses: "Go to the people and consecrate them today and tomorrow. Have them wash their clothes ¹¹and prepare for the third day, because on the third day the LORD will come down upon Mount Sinai in the sight of all the people. ¹²You shall set limits for the people all around, saying, 'Be careful not to go up the mountain or to touch the edge of it. Any who touch the mountain shall be put to death. ¹³No hand shall touch them, but they shall be stoned or shot with arrows; whether animal or human being, they shall not live.' When the trumpet sounds a long blast, they may go up on the mountain." ¹⁴So Moses went down from the mountain to the people. He consecrated the people, and they washed their clothes. [15]And he said to the people, "Prepare for the third day; **do not go near a woman.**"

[16]On the morning of the third day there was thunder and lightning, as well as a thick cloud on the mountain, and a blast of a trumpet so loud that all the people who were in the camp trembled. [17]Moses brought the people out of the camp to meet God. They took their stand at the foot of the mountain. [18]Now Mount Sinai was wrapped in smoke, because the LORD had descended upon it in fire; the smoke went up like the smoke of a kiln, while the whole mountain shook violently. [19]As the blast of the trumpet grew louder and louder, Moses would speak and God would answer him in thunder. [20]When the LORD descended upon Mount Sinai, to the top of the mountain, the LORD summoned Moses to the top of the mountain, and Moses went up. [21]Then the LORD said to Moses, "Go down and warn the people not to break through to the LORD to look; otherwise many of them will perish. [22]Even the priests who approach the LORD must consecrate themselves or the LORD will break out against them." [23]Moses said to the LORD, "The people are not permitted to come up to Mount Sinai; for you yourself warned us, saying, 'Set limits around the mountain and keep it holy.'" [24]The LORD said to him, "Go down, and come up bringing **Aaron** with you; but do not let either the priests

do not go near a woman

The Bible sometimes infers that sexual activity can cause one to become temporarily ritually unclean (see for example Leviticus 15:18).

Aaron

the brother of Moses

or the people break through to come up to the LORD; otherwise he will break out against them." ²⁵So Moses went down to the people and told them.

Chapter 20

The Ten Commandments

¹Then God spoke all these words:

²I am the LORD your God, who brought you out of the land of Egypt, out of the house of slavery; ³you shall have no other gods before me.

⁴You shall not make for yourself an idol, whether in the form of anything that is in heaven above, or that is on the earth beneath, or that is in the water under the earth. ⁵You shall not bow down to them or worship them; for I the LORD your God am a jealous God, punishing children for the iniquity of parents, to the third and the fourth generation of those who reject me, ⁶but showing steadfast love to the thousandth generation of those who love me and keep my commandments.

⁷You shall not make wrongful use of the name of the LORD your God, for the LORD will not acquit anyone who misuses his name.

⁸Remember the sabbath day, and keep it holy. ⁹Six days you shall labor and do all your work. ¹⁰But the seventh day is a sabbath to the LORD your God; you shall not do any work—you, your son or your daughter, your male or female slave, your livestock, or the alien resident in your towns. ¹¹For in six days the LORD made heaven and earth, the sea,

> **murder**
> The Hebrew word can also mean "kill" in a more general sense.

and all that is in them, but rested the seventh day; therefore the LORD blessed the sabbath day and consecrated it.

¹²Honor your father and your mother, so that your days may be long in the land that the LORD your God is giving you.

¹³You shall not **murder.**

¹⁴You shall not commit adultery.

¹⁵You shall not steal.

¹⁶You shall not bear false witness against your neighbor.

¹⁷You shall not covet your neighbor's house; you shall not covet your neighbor's wife, or male or female slave, or ox, or donkey, or anything that belongs to your neighbor.

¹⁸When all the people witnessed the thunder and lightning, the sound of the trumpet, and the mountain smoking, they were afraid and trembled and stood at a distance, ¹⁹and said to Moses, "You speak to us, and we will listen; but do not let God speak to us, or we will die." ²⁰Moses said to the people, "Do not be afraid; for God has come only to test you and to put the fear of him upon you so that you do not sin." ²¹Then the people stood at a distance, while Moses drew near to the thick darkness where God was.

The Law Concerning the Altar

²²The LORD said to Moses: Thus you shall say to the Israelites: "You have seen for yourselves that I spoke with you from heaven. ²³You shall not make gods of silver alongside me, nor shall you make for yourselves gods of gold. ²⁴You need

make for me only an altar of earth and sacrifice on it your burnt offerings and your offerings of well-being, your sheep and your oxen; in every place where I cause my name to be remembered I will come to you and bless you. [25]But if you make for me an altar of stone, do not build it of hewn stones; for if you use a chisel upon it you profane it. [26]You shall not go up by steps to my altar, so that your nakedness may not be exposed on it."

Excerpt from *Pirke Aboth: Sayings of the Fathers*

edited with translations and commentaries by Isaac Unterman

MISHNA TWELVE

Hillel and Shammai received [the tradition] from them [from the preceding]. Hillel said: Be of the disciples of Aaron, loving peace and pursuing peace, loving thy fellow creatures, and drawing them near to the Torah.

Hillel and Shammai were the last of the five "**pairs.**" They lived in the first century before

> **pairs**
> Four pairs of rabbis preceded Hillel and Shammai; the first of the pairs (Jose ben Jochanan and Jose ben Joezer) flourished during the middle of the second century BC.

Talmud

extensive set of religious writings based on the Mishna but greatly expanded upon through the added commentary by rabbis of the third through the beginning of the sixth centuries

Gemara

rabbinic commentary as contained in the Talmud

destruction of the Temple

The Romans destroyed the Jerusalem Temple in AD 70.

the common era. The **Talmud** tells us that Hillel lived 120 years, but this has not been historically ascertained. Incidentally, another **Gemara** (Sabbath, 15a) tells us that the lives of Hillel, Simeon, Gamaliel, and his son Simeon, together accounted for one hundred years up to the **destruction of the Temple.** Special prominence has always surrounded the fifth and last of the "pairs." In distinction to the other eight personages, whose role in the literature of the Law is strictly circumscribed, the work of Hillel and Shammai has left an indelible mark throughout the breadth and depth of the talmudic ocean. They are practically the main pillars upon which the entire structure of the Talmudic Law has been erected, and the world of talmudic scholars draws its nourishment from them. Without them we can hardly envisage what character the Mishna and the Gemara might have taken.

Through his fine character, limitless modesty, endless patience, and wonderful tenderness for all human beings, Hillel soon became a legendary character. All sorts of stories and legends have sprung up around his personality and quickly spread from generation to generation.

Hillel became famous, as the Talmud tells us, in the following way. Once the **Benei Bethirah,** about whom we know practically nothing, asked Hillel whether it was necessary to make the **Passover sacrifice** if Passover Eve falls on **Sabbath.** Hillel answered in the affirmative and based his opinion upon accepted texts. The scholars, however, were not convinced and argued that they could not trust anyone who came from **Babylonia.** Hillel then said: "I heard this opinion from my teachers Shemaiah and Abtalion." This finally convinced the other scholars. Hillel's decision was accepted and he was appointed president of the **Sanhedrin** (Pesachim, 66a).

This story shows how strong the power of tradition was rooted even in those days. Whatever our ancestors did was sufficient precedent for doing the very same thing.

Benei Bethirah
Hebrew, "sons of Bethirah," about whom, as Unterman notes, we know practically nothing.

Passover sacrifice
In Hillel's time a lamb or kid was sacrificed at Passover in commemoration of the salvation of the Israelites during the tenth plague on Egypt (see Exodus 12:1–32).

Sabbath
sundown on Friday to sundown on Saturday, a day set aside for rest and religious celebration

Babylonia
Mesopotamian land to which many Israelites were taken into exile in the sixth century BC, thus establishing a large community that thrived for centuries; Hillel was Babylonian

Sanhedrin
assembly of seventy-one Jewish judges that served as supreme court and legislative body on behalf of the ancient Jewish community

"Love thy neighbor as you would thyself"
See Leviticus 19:18.

Prosbul
a legal procedure introduced by Hillel that allowed Jews to take out loans without the lender having to fear that the obligation to repay would be erased within the seven years of a "sabbatical year" (as was inferred from Deuteronomy 15:1–2)

B.C.E.
"before the common era," a common scholarly designation used in place of BC ("before Christ")

Hillel of Babylonia is one of the most brilliant talmudic lights, and personifies most perfectly the great ideal of uncompromising love for mankind. How much worldly wisdom is embodied in his wonderful stroke of genius to transform the positive but utopian dictum, **"Love thy neighbor as you would thyself,"** into the negative but realizable, "Do not unto others what is distasteful unto you!" Hillel possessed almost superhuman patience and faith. Nevertheless, they did not blind him to the concrete needs of daily life, just as his unlimited respect for the laws of the Torah did not prevent him from modifying them to make them more relevant to changing needs. How much wisdom there is in his creation of the fictional **"Prosbul,"** which nominally does not abolish the law of "Shemitah" (the law that a loan was wiped out after seven years), but circumvents it entirely!

Hillel was born in Babylonia in the year 75 **B.C.E.** His brother, Shebna, was a wealthy merchant and wanted Hillel to become a partner in his business. Hillel declined the offer, however, and chose instead the career of a scholar (Sotah, 21a).

The study of the **Torah** in this period was apparently not pursued very diligently, and the **yeshivas** in Babylonia—if such existed at all—were not held in great esteem. Judaism as a religious creed, on the other hand, was maintained on a high spiritual level. The Sabbath was strictly observed, and the **annual Temple tax,** as well as gifts and sacrifices, was regularly sent to Jerusalem. But the study of the Torah was perfunctory since the Babylonian Jews were in this respect dependent upon Palestine:

Yet even in Palestine the study of the Torah was much neglected. **Herod's tyrannical reign** was greatly responsible

Torah
in this context, the first five books of the Hebrew Bible (Genesis, Exodus, Leviticus, Numbers, Deuteronomy)

yeshivas
schools devoted mainly to the study of rabbinic literature

annual Temple tax
Jews were required by biblical law (see Exodus 30:13) to pay half a shekel as an offering for the Jerusalem Temple.

Herod's tyrannical reign
Herod the Great was king of the Jews from 37 BC to 4 BC; the Romans established and supported his reign, which was marked by unsettled relations with the Jewish people.

for this, and with the death of Shemaiah and Abtalion the light of the Torah was almost extinguished. The rise of Hillel, the continuator of the Torah in this generation, was therefore almost a miracle (Succah, 20a).

Hillel left his homeland, Babylonia, and came to Palestine to study at the feet of Shemaiah and Abtalion. In order to exist Hillel became a laborer. During the first half of the day he worked hard in order to eke out a miserable existence. The rest of the day he spent in study. Once it happened that he could not pay the house-guard and therefore could not enter the Yeshiva. But since he did not wish to miss the wise words of these two famous **Tanaim,** he climbed up upon the roof of the Yeshiva, although it was cold and snowing outside, and listened in to the class through the skylight. The snow covered him up completely, and thus he lay frozen throughout the night. The next morning, when the students gathered, they noticed that no light came from the skylight. It was then that Hillel was discovered upon the roof and taken down. He was thoroughly washed, rubbed with ointment, and placed near a fire to warm himself. This happened on a Sabbath, but the elders of the Yeshiva decreed that in honor of such a man it was permissible to violate the strict regulations of the Sabbath (Yoma, 35b).

Even while in Babylonia Hillel had achieved high standing, but he and the other scholars could never feel certain that their interpretation was consonant with the decisions of the Tanaim in Palestine. Hillel undoubtedly had many such doubts, but the Talmud tells us about three cases for

> **Tanaim**
> rabbis of the period AD 70 – 200, whose teachings are recorded in the Mishna

which Hillel undertook the dangerous voyage to Palestine at a time when the country was in a state of unrest and one's life was not safe.

One case concerns the cleanliness and uncleanliness of a leper (Siphra, chapter 9). The second case deals with the question whether it is permissible to eat **Matzoth** made of newly threshed wheat. The third case concerns sacrifices during festivals (Jerusalem Pesachim, chapter 6, **Halacha** 1.)

Matzoth
plural of *matzo*, unleavened bread that is eaten during the eight days of Passover

Halacha
(variant spellings: halachah, halakha, halakhah) Jewish law, either as the collective body or as a specific regulation or custom

The Babylonian scholars very often were in doubt as regards their own interpretation. As a result of this they were in a difficult position. They were never sure whether or not their decisions would be adhered to, as on many occasions the Halacha in Palestine was at variance with that in Babylonia. To be sure, Hillel's interpretation did invariably square with the Palestinian. But to avoid uncertainties he left for Palestine to acquaint himself with the decisions on the spot.

Hillel did not spend much time in Palestine on his first visit. He soon returned to Babylonia, but later, when the tyrannical rule of Herod slackened somewhat, he again returned to Palestine.

The Talmud and the **Midrash** tell many stories illustrating Hillel's amazing learning. Thus it is told that he knew all the seventy languages of the world, and the language of all the beasts, trees and plants, hills and valleys.

Midrash
Jewish interpretation of biblical passages; here, the term refers to the collection of such interpretations produced during the first several centuries AD, and comprising an important part of rabbinic literature

A rabbi was standing
This story told in the Talmud relates to the first phrase in the saying of Mishna Twelve: "Be of the disciples of Aaron . . ."

Elijah the Prophet
biblical figure featured in the books of Kings.

The chief traits of Hillel's character were his kindness and modesty, and the Talmud tells many charming stories on this score. His modest character grew out of his profound moral conscience and deep understanding. The main idea running through all his work is human fellowship. Religion to him is merely a means to achieve this end.

Hillel was the first of the Tanaim to make love for one's fellow man the mainspring of the Jewish religion. Once, when a gentile came to him and asked to teach him the entire Torah in one sentence, Hillel told him: "What is distasteful unto you, you should not do unto others. This is the entire Torah and the rest is merely an elaboration of this virtue. As you will study the Torah you will find that out for yourself" (Sabbath, 31a). . . .

A rabbi was standing in the market place when **Elijah the Prophet** appeared to him. The rabbi asked Elijah: "Is there anybody in this market place who will have a share in the **World to Come?**"

Elijah answered there was not. In the meanwhile there came two men, and Elijah said: "These two men will have a share in the World to Come."

The rabbi thereupon asked the two men: "What is your occupation?"

They answered: "We are merrymakers; whenever we see men quarreling we make peace between them" (Taanith, 22a).

World to Come
phrase commonly used in rabbinic texts to refer to the hereafter

Midrash Samuel
Midrash is a form of rabbinic study and writing, featuring interpretation of biblical texts (in this case, of the books of Samuel).

LOVING PEACE AND PURSUING PEACE. Not only is it necessary to love peace, but one must strive for it, hanker for it, use all available resources to achieve it.

The "**Midrash Samuel**" asserts that Hillel intended to suggest that we should take a lesson from Aaron, who by his service in the Temple sought to bring peace to mankind.

LOVING THY FELLOW CREATURES. The Hebrew text uses the word "Brioth"—creatures in general—to indicate that we must not merely love every human being but every living thing that God created.

Thus spake God unto Israel: "Children of Mine, what then do I demand of you? I demand of you that you shall love one another."

Rabbi Simeon ben Eleaser said: The remark "love thy

Rabbi Simeon ben Eleaser
a rabbi of the second century AD whose teachings are included in the Mishna

neighbor as thou would thyself" was accompanied by the oath: "I have created man and if you love him I am prepared to reward you munificently. And if you do not love him, I am a just judge and shall punish you severely" (Aboth de Rabbi Nathan, chapter XVI).

Our wise men have taught us: It is said in the Torah "You should not hate your brother in your heart. From that we infer that even hatred borne in one's heart is a crime" (Arechin, 16b).

Akiba said of the command "Thou shalt love thy neighbor as thyself" (Leviticus 19:18) that it was a fundamental principle of the Torah (Jerusalem, Nedarim IX).

What message did the Torah bring to Israel? Take up yourselves the yoke of the kingdom of heaven, vie one with the other in the fear of God and practice loving deeds toward one another (Siphre Deuteronomy, Section 323).

One may not disturb the mind of his fellow creatures, not even a **Gentile** (Chullin, 94a).

More serious is stealing from a Gentile than from a Jew because it involves in addition profaning the Heavenly Name (Tosephta Baba Kamma X, 15).

Our rabbis have taught: We must support the poor of the Gentiles with the poor of Israel; visit the sick of the Gentiles with the sick of Israel; and give honorable burial to the dead of the Gentiles as to the dead of Israel (Gittin, 61a).

Akiba
a rabbi whose teachings are included in the Mishna; he died as a martyr at the hand of the Romans in AD 132

Gentile
a non-Jew, from the Latin term meaning "nation"

Who is mighty? He who turns an enemy into his friend (Aboth de Rabbi Nathan, chapter XXIII).

Excerpt from *The Family Markowitz*

by Allegra Goodman

Ed always leads the seder. Sol and Estelle love the way he does it because he is so knowledgeable. Ed's area of expertise is the Middle East, so he ties Passover to the present day. And he is eloquent. They are very proud of their son-in-law.

"This is our festival of freedom," Ed says, "commemorating our liberation from slavery." He picks up a piece of matzo and reads from his **New Revised Haggadah:** "'This is the bread which our fathers and mothers ate in Mitzrayim when they were slaves.'" He adds from the translator's note: "'We use the Hebrew wold *Mitzrayim* to denote the ancient land of Egypt—'"

"As opposed to modern-day Mitzrayim," Miriam says dryly.

"'To differentiate it from modern Egypt,'" Ed reads. Then he puts down the matzo and extemporizes. "We eat this matzo so we will never forget what slavery is, and

> **New Revised Haggadah**
> The Haggadah (Hebrew, "telling") narrates the celebration of the Passover seder; it is based on the Book of Exodus. Miriam Markowitz later is shown reading the Orthodox Birnbaum Haggadah. The two editions used by Ed and Miriam reflect their liberal and orthodox leanings, respectively.

so that we continue to empathize with afflicted peoples throughout the world: those torn apart by civil wars, those starving or homeless, those crippled by poverty and disease. We think of the people oppressed for their religious or political beliefs. In particular, we meditate on the people in our own country who have not yet achieved full freedom; those discriminated against because of their race, gender, or sexual preference. We think of the subtle forms of slavery as well as the obvious ones—the gray areas that are now coming to light: sexual harassment, verbal abuse—" He can't help noticing Miriam as he says this. It's obvious that she is ignoring him. She is sitting there chanting to herself out of her Orthodox Birnbaum Haggadah and it offends him. "Finally, we turn to the world's hot spot—the Middle East," Ed says. "We think of war-torn Israel and pray for compromises. We consider the Palestinians, who have no land to call their own, and we call for moderation and perspective. As we sit around the seder table, we look to the past to give us insight into the present."

"Beautiful," murmurs Estelle. But Ed looks down unhappily to where the kids are sitting. Ben has his feet up on Yehudit's empty chair, and Avi is playing with Amy's hair. Miriam is still poring over her Haggadah.

"It's time for the four questions," he says sharply. . . .

"Now I'm going to answer the questions." He reads: "'We do these things to commemorate our slavery in Mitzrayim. For if God had not brought us out of slavery, we and all future generations would still be enslaved. We eat matzo because our ancestors did not have time to let their bread rise when they left E—Mitzrayim. We eat bitter herbs to remind us of the bitterness of slavery. We dip greens in salt water to remind us of our tears, and we recline at the table because we are free men and women.' Okay." . . .

Ed speeds on, plowing through the Haggadah. "'The ten plagues that befell the Egyptians: Blood, frogs, vermin, wild beasts, **murrain,** boils, hail, locusts, darkness, death of the firstborn.'" He looks up from his book and says, "We think of the suffering of the Egyptians as they faced these calamities. We are grateful for our deliverance, but we remember that the oppressor was also oppressed." He pauses there, struck by his own phrase. It's very good. "We cannot celebrate at the expense of others, nor can we say that we are truly free until the other oppressed peoples of the world are also free. We make common cause with all peoples and all minorities. Our struggle is their struggle, and their struggle is our struggle. We turn now to the blessing over the wine and the matzo. Then"—he nods to Estelle—"we'll be ready to eat."

"Daddy," Miriam says.

"Yes."

"This is ridiculous. This seder is getting shorter every year."

"We're doing it the same way we always do it," Ed tells her.

"No, you're not. It's getting shorter and shorter. It was short enough to begin with! You always skip the most important parts."

"Miriam!" Sarah hushes her.

"Why do we have to spend the whole time talking about minorities?" she asks. "Why are you always talking about civil rights?"

> **murrain**
> a disease of cattle

"Because that's what Passover is about," Sol tells her.

"Oh, okay, fine," Miriam says.

"Time for the **gefilte fish,**" Estelle announces. Amy gets up to help her, and the two of them bring in the salad plates. Each person has a piece of fish on a bed of lettuce with two cherry tomatoes and a dab of magenta horseradish sauce.

gefilte fish

traditional Jewish food, often served at the Passover seder

For Reflection

1. "Now therefore, if you obey my voice and keep my covenant . . ." (Exodus 19:5). Based on Exodus, chapters 19–20, what is the "covenant"? What rights and responsibilities do the Israelites take on due to their consenting to the Covenant (and thus to become God's Chosen People)?

2. Among the Ten Commandments, which ones could be considered relevant only for the ancient Israelites or for the Jews or Christians who follow the biblical tradition? Which ones could be said to be universally relevant, setting ethical principles that all people should live by?

3. "What is distasteful unto you, you should not do unto others." Compare the content and circumstances of Rabbi Hillel's statement with the Golden Rule, found in Matthew 7:12. How are they similar? How do they differ?

4. Review the actual saying of Mishna Twelve, as cited at the beginning of the excerpt from Pirke Aboth. Based on your reading of the rest of the excerpt, summarize the rabbinic perspective on these ideals of "loving."

5. In leading the seder celebration, what modern issues or concerns does Ed Markowitz emphasize? Explain why you think he emphasizes these modern issues or concerns as part of the Passover.

Chapter 10

Christianity

If you were to ask any of the world's two billion Christians what is essential to Christianity, the likely answer would include something about having faith in the teachings and the saving power of Jesus Christ. The New Testament, especially the four Gospels, presents Christ's teachings and explains in various passages the significance of the Crucifixion and Resurrection of Christ for the salvation of Christians. The New Testament also makes clear that to be a Christian is to have faith in Christ. We have included readings from Saint Augustine and Søren Kierkegaard, two Christians who eloquently expressed and explained their Christian faith. To begin, though, we start with the New Testament's Sermon on the Mount.

The Gospel of Matthew is the first book in the New Testament. The Sermon on the Mount (chapters 5–7) presents Jesus setting forth many of Christianity's foundational and most famous tenets. The Beatitudes, the teachings to "turn the other cheek" and to "love your enemies," the injunction against judging others, the Golden Rule, the Lord's Prayer— all are bedrock elements of Christianity.

Saint Augustine (AD 354–430) is considered to be one of the greatest Christian philosophers. His many works, the most famous of which are the *City of God* and *Confessions*, form an intellectual bridge from the classical Roman world to the European Middle Ages. It is clear in *Confessions*, however, that Augustine, in his early life, explored divergent religious paths before becoming a Christian. According to Augustine's own description in Book VIII.12 of his conversion to Christianity, he harbored doubts about becoming a Christian up to the final moment. Remarkably introspective and personal, *Confessions* recounts Augustine's experiences and attitudes that led eventually to his conversion to Christianity.

Danish philosopher Søren Kierkegaard (1813–1855) is among the most influential figures in the history of Protestant Christianity. *The Concluding Unscientific Postscript to Philosophical Fragments*, from which our excerpt is drawn, is his most important work. Passionately refuting the notion that Christianity can be sufficiently understood through objective or abstract philosophy, Kierkegaard insists that the decision to be a Christian is a matter of inwardness, or subjectivity. As he famously puts it, "Truth is subjectivity"—to be a Christian is to be in a faith relationship with God that is entirely unique to the individual. In the challenging passage excerpted here, Kierkegaard examines various possibilities for determining whether one is a Christian based on objective facts—for example, whether one has been baptized. He rejects such possibilities, concluding instead that all depends on the inner quality of the individual's faith: "not by the 'what' of Christianity but by the 'how' of the Christian."

Matthew, Chapters 5–7

Chapter 5

The Sermon on the Mount

¹When Jesus saw the crowds, he went up the mountain; and after he sat down, his disciples came to him. ²Then he began to speak, and taught them, saying:

The Beatitudes

³"Blessed are the poor in spirit, for theirs is the **kingdom of heaven.**

⁴"Blessed are those who mourn, for they will be comforted.

⁵"Blessed are the meek, for they will inherit the earth.

⁶"Blessed are those who hunger and thirst for righteousness, for they will be filled.

⁷"Blessed are the merciful, for they will receive mercy.

⁸"Blessed are the pure in heart, for they will see God.

⁹"Blessed are the peacemakers, for they will be called children of God.

¹⁰"Blessed are those who are persecuted for righteousness' sake, for theirs is the kingdom of heaven.

kingdom of heaven
The coming of the kingdom of heaven (in other Gospels the term *kingdom of God* is used), or Reign of God, is a primary theme of Jesus's ministry.

[11]"Blessed are you when people revile you and persecute you and utter all kinds of evil against you falsely on my account. [12]Rejoice and be glad, for your reward is great in heaven, for in the same way they persecuted the prophets who were before you.

Salt and Light

[13]"You are the salt of the earth; but if salt has lost its taste, how can its saltiness be restored? It is no longer good for anything, but is thrown out and trampled under foot.

[14] "You are the light of the world. A city built on a hill cannot be hid. [15]No one after lighting a lamp puts it under the bushel basket, but on the lampstand, and it gives light to all in the house. [16]In the same way, let your light shine before others, so that they may see your good works and give glory to your Father in heaven.

The Law and the Prophets

[17] "Do not think that I have come to abolish the law or the prophets; I have come not to abolish but to fulfill. [18]For truly I tell you, until heaven and earth pass away, not one letter, not one stroke of a letter, will pass from the law until all is accomplished. [19]Therefore, whoever breaks one of the least of these commandments, and teaches others to do the same, will be called least in the kingdom of heaven; but whoever does them and teaches them will be called great in the kingdom of heaven. [20]For I tell you, unless your righteousness exceeds that of the **scribes and Pharisees,** you will never enter the kingdom of heaven.

Concerning Anger

scribes and Pharisees
a common reference
in Matthew to Jewish
scholarly authorities;
the Pharisees eventually
emerged as the primary
founders of rabbinic, or
classical, Judaism

[21]"You have heard that it was said to those of ancient times, 'You shall not murder'; and 'whoever murders shall be liable to judgment.' [22]But I say to you that if you are angry with a brother or sister, you will be liable to judgment; and if you insult a brother or sister, you will be liable to the council; and if you say, 'You fool,' you will be liable to the hell of fire. [23]So when you are offering your gift at the altar, if you remember that your brother or sister has something against you, [24]leave your gift there before the altar and go; first be reconciled to your brother or sister, and then come and offer your gift. [25]Come to terms quickly with your accuser while you are on the way to court with him, or your accuser may hand you over to the judge, and the judge to the guard, and you will be thrown into prison. [26]Truly I tell you, you will never get out until you have paid the last penny.

Concerning Adultery

[27]"You have heard that it was said, 'You shall not commit adultery.' [28]But I say to you that everyone who looks at a woman with lust has already committed adultery with her in his heart. [29]If your right eye causes you to sin, tear it out and throw it away; it is better for you to lose one of your members than for your whole body to be thrown into hell. [30]And if your right hand causes you to sin, cut it off and throw it

away; it is better for you to lose one of your members than for your whole body to go into hell.

Concerning Divorce

31"It was also said, 'Whoever divorces his wife, let him give her a **certificate of divorce.**' 32But I say to you that anyone who divorces his wife, except on the ground of unchastity, causes her to commit adultery; and whoever marries a divorced woman commits adultery.

certificate of divorce
a reference to the biblical law (see Deuteronomy 24:1–4)

Concerning Oaths

33"Again, you have heard that it was said to those of ancient times, 'You shall not swear falsely, but carry out the vows you have made to the Lord.' 34But I say to you, Do not swear at all, either by heaven, for it is the throne of God, 35or by the earth, for it is his footstool, or by Jerusalem, for it is the city of the great King. 36And do not swear by your head, for you cannot make one hair white or black. 37Let your word be 'Yes, Yes' or 'No, No'; anything more than this comes from the **evil one.**

evil one
The Greek term can also be translated simply as "evil."

Concerning Retaliation

38"You have heard that it was said, 'An eye for an eye and a tooth for a tooth.' 39But I say to you, Do not resist an evildoer. But if anyone strikes you on the right cheek, turn the other also; 40and if anyone wants to sue you and take your coat, give your cloak as well; ⁴¹and if anyone forces you to go one mile, go also the second mile. ⁴²Give to everyone who begs from you, and do not refuse anyone who wants to borrow from you.

Love for Enemies

⁴³"You have heard that it was said, 'You shall love your neighbor and hate your enemy.' ⁴⁴But I say to you, Love your enemies and pray for those who persecute you, ⁴⁵so that you may be children of your Father in heaven; for he makes his sun rise on the evil and on the good, and sends rain on the righteous and on the unrighteous. ⁴⁶For if you love those who love you, what reward do you have? Do not even the tax-collectors do the same? ⁴⁷And if you greet only your brothers and sisters, what more are you doing than others? Do not even the Gentiles do the same? ⁴⁸Be perfect, there-fore, as your heavenly Father is perfect.

Chapter 6

Concerning Almsgiving

¹"Beware of practicing your piety before others in order to be seen by them; for then you have no reward from your Father in heaven.

²"So **whenever you give alms,** do not sound a trumpet before you, as the hypocrites do in the synagogues and in the streets, so that they may be praised by others. Truly I tell you, they have received their reward. ³But when you give

alms, do not let your left hand know what your right hand is doing, [4]so that your alms may be done in secret; and your Father who sees in secret will reward you.

> **whenever you give alms**
> Alms, or charitable gifts, were donated on the Sabbath in synagogues.

Concerning Prayer

[5]"And whenever you pray, do not be like the hypocrites; for they love to stand and pray in the synagogues and at the street corners, so that they may be seen by others. Truly I tell you, they have received their reward. [6]But whenever you pray, go into your room and shut the door and pray to your Father who is in secret; and your Father who sees in secret will reward you.

[7]"When you are praying, do not heap up empty phrases as the Gentiles do; for they think that they will be heard because of their many words. [8]Do not be like them, for your Father knows what you need before you ask him.

[9]"Pray then in this way:
Our Father in heaven,
    hallowed be your name.
    [10]Your kingdom come.
    Your will be done,
        on earth as it is in heaven.
[11]Give us this day our daily bread.
[12]And forgive us our debts,
    as we also have forgiven our debtors.
[13]And do not bring us to the time of trial,
    but rescue us from the evil one.

[14]For if you forgive others their trespasses, your heavenly Father will also forgive you; [15]but if you do not forgive others, neither will your Father forgive your trespasses.

Concerning Fasting

[16]"And **whenever you fast,** do not look dismal, like the hypocrites, for they disfigure their faces so as to show others that they are fasting. Truly I tell you, they have received their reward. [17]But when you fast, put oil on your head and wash your face, [18]so that your fasting may be seen not by others but by your Father who is in secret; and your Father who sees in secret will reward you.

whenever you fast
Jews were required to fast once per year, on Yom Kippur (the Day of Atonement); some also fasted on other occasions.

Concerning Treasures

[19]"Do not store up for yourselves treasures on earth, where moth and rust consume and where thieves break in and steal; [20]but store up for yourselves treasures in heaven, where neither moth nor rust consumes and where thieves do not break in and steal. [21]For where your treasure is, there your heart will be also.

The Sound Eye

[22]"The eye is the lamp of the body. So, if your eye is healthy, your whole body will be full of light; [23]but if your eye is unhealthy, your whole body will be full of darkness. If then the light in you is darkness, how great is the darkness!

Serving Two Masters

24"No one can serve two masters; for a slave will either hate the one and love the other, or be devoted to the one and despise the other. You cannot serve God and wealth.

Do Not Worry

25"Therefore I tell you, do not worry about your life, what you will eat or what you will drink, or about your body, what you will wear. Is not life more than food, and the body more than clothing? 26Look at the birds of the air; they neither sow nor reap nor gather into barns, and yet your heavenly Father feeds them. Are you not of more value than they? 27And can any of you by worrying add a single hour to your span of life? 28And why do you worry about clothing? Consider the lilies of the field, how they grow; they neither toil nor spin, 29yet I tell you, even **Solomon** in all his glory was not clothed like one of these. 30But if God so clothes the grass of the field, which is alive today and tomorrow is thrown into the oven, will he not much more clothe you—you of little faith? 31Therefore do not worry, saying, 'What will we eat?' or 'What will we drink?' or 'What will we wear?' 32For it is the Gentiles who strive for all these things; and indeed your heavenly Father knows that you need all these things. 33But strive first for the kingdom of God and his righteousness, and all these things will be given to you as well.

34"So do not worry about tomorrow, for tomorrow will bring worries of its own. Today's trouble is enough for today.

> **Solomon**
> the biblical king, son of David, who was famous for his glorious splendor (see 1 Kings, chapter 10)

Chapter 7

Judging Others

[1]"Do not judge, so that you may not be judged. [2]For with the judgment you make you will be judged, and the measure you give will be the measure you get. [3]Why do you see the speck in your neighbor's eye, but do not notice the log in your own eye? [4]Or how can you say to your neighbor, 'Let me take the speck out of your eye,' while the log is in your own eye? [5]You hypocrite, first take the log out of your own eye, and then you will see clearly to take the speck out of your neighbor's eye.

Profaning the Holy

[6]"Do not give what is holy to dogs; and do not throw your pearls before swine, or they will trample them under foot and turn and maul you.

Ask, Search, Knock

[7]"Ask, and it will be given to you; search, and you will find; knock, and the door will be opened for you. [8]For everyone who asks receives, and everyone who searches finds, and for everyone who knocks, the door will be opened. [9]Is there anyone among you who, if your child asks for bread, will give a stone? [10]Or if the child asks for a fish, will give a snake? [11]If you then, who are evil, know how to give good gifts to your children, how much more will your Father in heaven give good things to those who ask him!

The Golden Rule

[12]"In everything do to others as you would have them do to you; for this is the law and the prophets.

The Narrow Gate

[13]"Enter through the narrow gate; for the gate is wide and the road is easy that leads to destruction, and there are many who take it. [14]For the gate is narrow and the road is hard that leads to life, and there are few who find it.

A Tree and Its Fruit

[15]"Beware of false prophets, who come to you in sheep's clothing but inwardly are ravenous wolves. [16]You will know them by their fruits. Are grapes gathered from thorns, or figs from thistles? [17]In the same way, every good tree bears good fruit, but the bad tree bears bad fruit. [18]A good tree cannot bear bad fruit, nor can a bad tree bear good fruit. [19]Every tree that does not bear good fruit is cut down and thrown into the fire. [20]Thus you will know them by their fruits.

Concerning Self-Deception

[21]"Not everyone who says to me, 'Lord, Lord,' will enter the kingdom of heaven, but only one who does the will of my Father in heaven. [22]On that day many will say to me, 'Lord, Lord, did we not prophesy in your name, and cast out demons in your name, and do many deeds of power in your name?' [23]Then I will declare to them, 'I never knew you; go away from me, you evildoers.'

Hearers and Doers

[24]"Everyone then who hears these words of mine and acts on them will be like a wise man who built his house on rock. [25]The rain fell, the floods came, and the winds blew and beat on that house, but it did not fall, because it had been founded on rock. [26]And everyone who hears these words of mine and does not act on them will be like a foolish man who built his house on sand. [27]The rain fell, and the floods came, and the winds blew and beat against that house, and it fell—and great was its fall!"

[28]Now when Jesus had finished saying these things, the crowds were astounded at his teaching, [29]for he taught them as one having authority, and not as their scribes.

Excerpt from *Confessions*

by Saint Augustine

I probed the hidden depths of my soul and wrung its pitiful secrets from it, and when I mustered them all before the eyes of my heart, a great storm broke within me, bringing with it a great deluge of tears. I stood up and left **Alypius** so that I might weep and cry to my heart's content, for it occurred to me that tears were best shed in solitude. I moved away far enough to avoid being embarrassed even by his presence.

Alypius
Augustine's friend

He must have realized what my feelings were, for I suppose I had said something and he had known from the sound of my voice that I was ready to burst into tears. So I stood up and left him where we had been sitting, utterly bewildered. Somehow I flung myself down beneath a fig tree and gave way to the tears which now streamed from my eyes, the sacrifice that is acceptable to you. I had much to say to you, my God, not in these very words but in this strain: *Lord, will you never be content? Must we always taste your vengeance? Forget the long record of our sins.* For I felt that I was still the captive of my sins, and in my misery I kept crying "How long shall I go on saying 'tomorrow, tomorrow'? Why not now? Why not make an end of my ugly sins at this moment?"

I was asking myself these questions, weeping all the while with the most bitter sorrow in my heart, when all at once I heard the sing-song voice of a child in a nearby house. Whether it was the voice of a boy or a girl I cannot say, but again and again it repeated the refrain, "Take it and read, take it and read." At this I looked up, thinking hard whether there was any kind of game in which children used to chant words like these, but I could not remember ever hearing them before. I stemmed my flood of tears and stood up, telling myself that this could only be a divine command to open my book of Scripture and read the first passage on which my eyes should fall.

For I had heard the story of **Antony,** and I remembered how he had happened to go into a church while the Gospel was being read and had taken it as a counsel addressed to himself when he

Antony
Augustine and Alypius have previously been told the story of the conversion of Saint Antony.

heard **the words** *Go home and sell all that belongs to you. Give it to the poor, and so the treasure you have shall be in heaven; then come back and follow me.* By this divine pronouncement he had at once been converted to you.

So I hurried back to the place where Alypius was sitting, for when I stood up to move away I had put down the book containing Paul's Epistles. I seized it and opened it, and in silence I read **the first passage** on which my eyes fell: *Not in revelling and drunkenness, not in lust and wantonness, not in quarrels and rivalries. Rather, arm yourselves with the Lord Jesus Christ; spend no more thought on nature and nature's appetites.* I had no wish to read more and no need to do so. For in an instant, as I came to the end of the sentence, it was as though the light of confidence flooded into my heart and all the darkness of doubt was dispelled.

I marked the place with my finger or by some other sign and closed the book. My looks now were quite calm as I told Alypius what had happened to me. He too told me what he had been feeling, which of course I did not know. He asked to see what I had read. I showed it to him and he read on beyond the text which I had read. I did not know what followed, but **it was this: *Find room*** *among you for a man of over-delicate conscience.* Alypius applied this to himself

---

the words *Go home*
Augustine cites Matthew 19:21.

the first passage
This refers to Romans 13:13–14.

it was this: *Find room*
This refers to Romans 14:1.

and told me so. This admonition was enough to give him strength, and without suffering the distress of hesitation he made his resolution and took this good purpose to himself. And it very well suited his moral character, which had long been far, far better than my own.

Then we went in and told **my mother,** who was overjoyed. And when we went on to describe how it had all happened, she was jubilant with triumph and glorified you, *who are powerful enough,* and more than powerful enough, to carry out your purpose beyond all our hopes and dreams. For she saw that you had granted her far more than she used to ask in her tearful prayers and plaintive lamentations. You converted me to yourself, so that I no longer desired a wife or placed any hope in this world but stood firmly upon the rule of faith, where you had shown me to her in a dream so many years before. And you *turned her sadness into rejoicing,* into joy far fuller than her dearest wish, far sweeter and more chaste than any she had hoped to find in children begotten of my flesh.

my mother
Saint Monica

who are powerful enough
Augustine cites Ephesians 3:20.

turned her sadness into rejoicing
Augustine refers to Psalm 30:11.

Excerpt from *Concluding Unscientific Postscript to Philosophical Fragments*

by Søren Kierkegaard

Becoming or Being a Christian Is Defined Objectively in the Following Way:

A Christian is one who accepts Christianity's doctrine. But if the "what" of this doctrine is to decide ultimately whether one is a Christian, then attention is immediately turned outward in order to find out what Christianity's doctrine is, down to the slightest detail, because this "what" is not to decide what Christianity is but whether I am a Christian.—At that very moment begins the learned, the uneasy, the timorous contradiction of approximating. The approximation can go on as long as it wants to, and because of it the decision by which the individual becomes a Christian is eventually forgotten completely.

This dubious situation has been remedied by the presupposition that everyone in Christendom is a Christian; we are all as such what people call Christians. The objective theories fare better with this presupposition. We are all Christians. The Bible theory now must examine with proper objectivity what Christianity indeed is (and yet, of course, we are Christians, and it is assumed that the objective knowledge will make us Christians, the objective knowledge that we will really come to have only now, we who are Christians—because if we are not Christians, the road taken here is the very one that will never lead to becoming Christians). The Church theory assumes that we are Christians, but now we must in a purely objective way have it made sure what the essentially Christian is in order to defend ourselves against the Turk and the Russian and the Roman yoke, and valiantly battle Christianity forward by having our age form a bridge, as it were, to a matchless future, which is already glimpsed. This is sheer estheticism. Christianity is an existence-communication. The task is to become a Christian or to continue to be a Christian, and the most dangerous illusion of all is to become so sure of being one that all Christendom must be defended against the Turk—instead of defending the faith within oneself against the illusion about the Turk.

No, it is said, not every acceptance of the Christian doctrine makes one a Christian. What it especially depends upon is appropriation, that one appropriates and holds fast this doctrine in a way entirely different from the way one holds anything else, that one will live and die in it, risk one's life for it, etc.

It seems as if this were something. The category "altogether different" is, however, a rather mediocre category, and the whole formula, which attempts to define being Christian somewhat more subjectively, is neither one thing nor the other, and in a way avoids the difficulty with the distraction and deceit of **approximation** but lacks the categorical qualification. The pathos of **appropriation** of which it speaks is the pathos of immediacy. One can just as well say that a rapturous lover relates himself to his erotic love in this way: he will hold it fast and appropriate it in a way entirely different from the way he holds anything else, will live in it and die in it, risk everything for it. So far there is no essential

approximation . . . appropriation

Kierkegaard insists here and throughout the following four paragraphs on the special uniqueness of being a Christian; when trying to understand these challenging concepts of approximation and appropriation, it is helpful to take note of the statement that concludes this section: "The appropriation by which a Christian is Christian must be so specific that it cannot be confused with anything else."

difference in inwardness between a lover and a Christian, and one is again obliged to return to the "what" that is the doctrine, and thus we again come under no.

1. . . .

Becoming and being a Christian are defined neither objectively by the "what" of the doctrine nor subjectively by the appropriation, not by what has taken place within the individual but by what has taken place with the individual: that the individual is baptized. Insofar as acceptance of the Creed is added to Baptism, nothing decisive is gained thereby, but the definition will vacillate between accentuating the "what" (the way of approximation) and talking vaguely about acceptance and acceptance and appropriation etc., without any specific qualification.

If being baptized is supposed to be the qualification, attention will immediately turn outward in deliberation on whether I actually have been baptized. Then begins the approximation with regard to a historical fact. . . .

Being a Christian Is Defined Subjectively in This Way:

The decision rests in the subject; the appropriation is the **paradoxical inwardness** that is specifically different from all other inwardness. Being a Christian is defined not by the "what" of Christianity but by the "how" of the Christian. This "how" can fit only one thing, the absolute paradox. Therefore there is no vague talk that being a Christian means to accept and accept, and accept altogether differently, to appropriate, to have faith, to appropriate in faith altogether differently (nothing but rhetorical and sham definitions); but to have faith is specifically qualified differently from all other appropriation and inwardness. **Faith is the objective uncertainty with the repulsion of the absurd,** held fast in the passion of inwardness, which is the relation of inwardness intensified to its highest. This formula fits

paradoxical inwardness
paradoxical, because faith is a deeply personal relationship with God that is unique to the individual, and yet God is the universal ground or source of truth for all individuals

Faith is the objective uncertainty with the repulsion of the absurd
For Kierkegaard, who elsewhere writes that to have faith is "to go to sea in a sieve," uncertainty and "the absurd" are inevitably involved because faith defies the logic of ordinary human experience; for Kierkegaard's fullest treatment of faith, see *Fear and Trembling,* in which he features Abraham's willingness to sacrifice Isaac as the perfect model of faith (this story is told in Genesis, chapter 22).

only the one who has faith, no one else, not even a lover, or an enthusiast, or a thinker, but solely and only the one who has faith, who relates himself to the absolute paradox.

For Reflection

1. In Matthew, chapter 5, the first chapter of the Sermon on the Mount, Jesus refers frequently to traditional Jewish teachings. Identify specific examples of how Jesus reinterprets or expands on these traditional teachings.

2. Review the following teachings from the Sermon on the Mount (Matthew, chapters 5–7). Explain how they relate to one another. How do you think modern society practices these principles? Explain and provide specific examples.
    a. 5:38–48: "turn the other cheek" and "love your enemies"
    b. 7:1–5: "Do not judge . . ."
    c. 7:12: the Golden Rule

3. Summarize the events leading up to Augustine's full conversion to Christian faith. Why do you think these events triggered his conversion experience?

4. Describe what you believe Augustine must have been thinking and feeling during the moment of his conversion and in its aftermath.

5. "Being a Christian is defined not by the 'what' of Christianity but by the 'how' of the Christian." Explain, in your own words, what you believe Kierkegaard is saying in this statement. Also explain why you agree or disagree with Kierkegaard.

Chapter 11

Islam

The basic principle of Islam is inferred in its very name, which is derived from an Arabic root word meaning "submission." A Muslim ("one who submits") is to submit to the will of the one God, Allah. Through our primary sources in this chapter, we explore various examples of the teachings and practices of Islam—all of them directly relating to this basic principle of submission to God.

The Qur'an, Islam's sacred text, is the primary means of knowing the will of God. It is believed to contain the direct revelations of Allah, transmitted to the Prophet Muhammad (about AD 570–632). It consists of 114 suras, or chapters, of varying length. We have chosen to include here the complete sura 22, titled "The Pilgrimage." The reader will note the variety of subjects addressed in the sura. Such diversity is common, as is the repetition of many of the most important ideas. Note, for example, the various ways by which the Qur'an refers to God, as "the Giver of Mercy," "Lord of the Worlds," "Master of the Day of Judgment," and so forth. Along with applying this array of names, the Qur'an insists repeatedly that there is one omnipotent God. Other important ideas that are featured in sura 22 include the "Day of Judgment"; the nature of the afterlife; the proper societal relations of Muslims to other groups, including Jews and

Christians; and the appropriateness of taking up arms for defensive purposes.

Abu Hamid Muhammad Al-Ghāzāli (1058–1111) is considered by many to be the greatest authority on Islamic theology since the Prophet Muhammad. In *The Faith and Practice of Al-Ghāzāli*, al-Ghāzāli offers an autobiographical account of his development as a Muslim practitioner and scholar. In our excerpts, he describes his experiences with Sufism, a widespread form of Islam that features mystical approaches to knowing and worshiping Allah. These experiences eventually led him to conclude "that it is above all the mystics who walk on the road of God . . ." In the pages preceding the excerpt featured in this chapter, al-Ghāzāli explains that although Sufism involves "both intellectual belief and practical activity," the crucial element is not something that can be "apprehended by study, but only by immediate experience, by ecstasy and by a moral change" (Watt, pages 56–57). Regarding "moral change," the reader who is familiar with Saint Augustine's *Confessions* (see chapter 10) will note that these two men had similar questions concerning their moral worthiness. The excerpt concludes with al-Ghāzāli's remarkable description of the inner experiences of one who is on the mystic "way"; ultimately, he says, words fail any attempt to explain these experiences adequately.

The story of the Tangouri family is the story of countless American families. They work to balance jobs, school, social obligations, and family time. They are also devoted to living their Islamic faith as completely as they can. In the reading, they share about the challenges they face and the support they encounter living their faith in America. As you read their account, consider how the Tangouri family is like families you know.

Excerpt from *The Qur'an*

Sura 22: The Pilgrimage

In the name of God, the Lord of Mercy, the Giver of Mercy

People, be mindful of your Lord, for the earthquake of the **Last Hour** will be a mighty thing: on the Day you see it, every nursing mother will think no more of her baby, every pregnant female will miscarry, you will think people are drunk when they are not, so severe will be God's torment. Yet still there are some who, with no knowledge, argue about God, who follow every devilish rebel fated to lead astray those who take his side, and guide them to the suffering of the blazing flame.

People, [remember,] if you doubt the **Resurrection,** that **We created** you from dust, then a drop of fluid, then a clinging form, then a lump of flesh, both shaped and unshaped: We mean to make Our power clear to you.

Last Hour
the anticipated time of God's intervention in history, at which time the dead will be resurrected and all will be judged

Resurrection
or "the Day of Resurrection," another reference to God's intervention in history

We created
The Qur'an often employs the first person plural ("we") when referring to Allah.

Whatever We choose We cause to remain in the womb for an appointed time, then We bring you forth as infants and then you grow and reach maturity. Some die young and some are left to live on to such an age that they forget all they once knew. You sometimes see the earth lifeless, yet when We send down water it stirs and swells and produces every kind of joyous growth: this is because God is the Truth; He brings the dead back to life; He has power over everything.

There is no doubt that the Last Hour is bound to come, nor that God will raise the dead from their graves, yet still there are some who, with no knowledge or guidance or any book of enlightenment, argue about God, turning scornfully aside to lead others away from God's path. Disgrace in this world awaits such a person and, on the Day of Resurrection, We shall make him taste the suffering of the Fire. [It will be said], "This is for what you have stored up with your own hands: God is never unjust to His creatures."

There are also some who serve God with unsteady faith: if something good comes their way, they are satisfied, but if they are tested, they revert to their old ways, losing both this world and the next—that is the clearest loss. Instead of God, they call upon what can neither harm nor help them—that is straying far away—or invoke one whose harm is closer than his help: an evil master and an evil companion. But God will admit those who believe and do good deeds to Gardens graced with flowing streams. God does whatever He wishes. Anyone who thinks that God will not support him in this world and the next should stretch a rope up to the sky, climb all the way up it, and see whether this strategy removes the cause of his anger. In this way, We send the Qur'an down as clear messages, and God guides whoever He will.

As for the believers, those who follow the Jewish faith, the **Sabians,** the Christians, the **Magians,** and the idolaters, God will judge between them on the Day of Resurrection; God witnesses all things. **Do you not realize [Prophet]** that everything in the heavens and earth submits to God: the sun, the moon, the stars, the mountains, the trees, and the animals? So do many human beings, though for many others punishment is well deserved. Anyone disgraced by God will have no one to honour him: God does whatever He will. These two kinds of people disagree about their Lord. Garments of fire will be tailored for those who

Sabians
a monotheistic religious community that is therefore regarded relatively favorably in the Qur'an

Magians
followers of the ancient Persian prophet Zarathustra and thus monotheists

Do you not realize [Prophet]
Here, and at numerous points elsewhere in the Qur'an, Allah addresses Muhammad directly, using the singular personal pronoun ("you").

disbelieve; scalding water will be poured over their heads, melting their insides as well as their skins; there will be iron crooks to restrain them; whenever, in their anguish, they try to escape, they will be pushed back in and told, "Taste the suffering of the Fire."' But God will admit those who believe and do good deeds to Gardens graced with flowing streams; there they will be adorned with golden bracelets and pearls; there they will have silken garments. They were guided to good speech and to the path of the One Worthy of all Praise.

As for the disbelievers, who bar others from God's path and from the **Sacred Mosque**—which We made for all people, residents and visitors alike—and who try to violate it with wrongdoing, We shall make them taste a painful punishment. **We showed Abraham the site of the House,** saying, "'Do not assign partners to Me. Purify My House for those who circle around it, those who stand to pray, and those who bow and prostrate themselves. Proclaim the **Pilgrimage** to all people. They will come to you on foot and on every kind of swift mount, emerging from every deep mountain pass to attain benefits and celebrate God's name, on specified days, over the livestock He has provided for them—feed yourselves and the poor and unfortunate—so let the pilgrims perform their acts of cleansing, fulfil their vows, and circle around the Ancient House." All this [is ordained by God]: anyone who honours the sacred ordinances of God will have good rewards from his Lord.

Sacred Mosque
the Kaaba, the sacred shrine of Mecca

We showed Abraham the site of the House
The "House" (or "Ancient House," as found a few sentences below) is the Kaaba, which, according to the Qur'an, Abraham and his son Ishmael built (see sura 2:125–127).

Pilgrimage
the *Hajj*; to make a pilgrimage to Mecca during the holy month of Ramadan once in a lifetime is one of the Five Pillars of Islam; Qur'anic passages such as this one instruct Muslims to this day as to how to perform the *Hajj*.

Livestock have been made lawful to you, except for what has been explicitly forbidden. Shun the filth of idolatrous beliefs and practices and shun false utterances. Devote yourselves to God and assign Him no partners, for the person who does so is like someone who has been hurled down from the skies and snatched up by the birds or flung to a distant place by the wind. All this [is ordained by God]: those who honour God's rites show the piety of their hearts. Livestock are useful to you until the set time. Then their place of sacrifice is near the Ancient House: We appointed acts of devotion for every community, for them to celebrate God's name over the livestock He provided for them: your God is One, so devote yourselves to Him. [Prophet], give good news to the humble whose hearts fill with awe whenever God is mentioned, who endure whatever happens to them with patience, who keep up the prayer, who give to others out of Our provision to them.

We have made camels part of God's sacred rites for you. There is much good in them for you, so invoke God's name over them as they are lined up for sacrifice, then, when they have fallen down dead, feed yourselves and those who do not ask, as well as those who do. We have subjected them to you in this way so that you may be thankful. It is neither their meat nor their blood that reaches God but your piety. He has subjected them to you in this way so that you may glorify God for having guided you.

Give good news to those who do good: God will defend the believers; God does not love the unfaithful or the ungrateful. Those who have been attacked are permitted to take up arms because they have been wronged—God has the power to help them—those who have been driven unjustly from their homes only for saying, "Our Lord is God." If God did not repel some people by means of others, many monasteries, churches, synagogues, and mosques, where God's name is much invoked, would have been destroyed. God is sure to help those who help His cause—God is strong and mighty—those who, when We establish them in the land, keep up the prayer, pay the prescribed alms, command what is right, and forbid what is wrong: God controls the outcome of all events.

If they reject you [Prophet], so did the people of Noah before them, and those of **'Ad, Thamud,** Abraham, Lot, **Midian.** Moses too was called a liar. I gave the disbelievers time, but in the end I punished them. How I condemned them! How many towns steeped in wrongdoing We have destroyed and left in total ruin; how many deserted wells; how many lofty palaces! Have these people [of Mecca] not travelled through the land with hearts to understand and ears to hear? It is not people's eyes that are blind, but their hearts within their breasts.

They will challenge you [Prophet] to hasten the punishment. God will not fail in His promise—a Day with your Lord is like a thousand years by your reckoning. To many a town steeped in wrongdoing I gave more time and then struck them down: they all return to Me in the end.

Say [Prophet], "People, I am sent only to give you clear warning." Those who believe and do good deeds will be forgiven and have a generous reward, but those who

'Ad, Thamud
men of ancient Arabia

Midian
the fourth son of Abraham, by his concubine Keturah (see Genesis 25:1–2)

strive to oppose Our messages and try in vain to defeat Us are destined for the Blaze. We have never sent any messenger or prophet before you [Muhammad] into whose wishes Satan did not insinuate something, but God removes what Satan insinuates and then God affirms His message. God is all knowing and wise: He makes Satan's insinuations a temptation only for the sick at heart and those whose hearts are hardened—the evildoers are profoundly opposed [to the Truth]—and He causes those given knowledge to realize that this Revelation is your Lord's Truth, so that they may believe in it and humble their hearts to Him: God guides the faithful to the straight path. The disbelievers will remain in doubt about it until the Hour suddenly overpowers them or until torment descends on them on a Day devoid of all hope. On that Day control will belong to God: He will judge between them. Those who believe and do good deeds will be admitted to Gardens of Delight, while those who disbelieve and reject Our revelations will receive a humiliating torment.

He will give a generous provision to those who migrated in God's way and were killed or died. He is the Best Provider. He will admit them to a place that will please them: God is all knowing and most forbearing. So it will be. God will help those who retaliate against an aggressive act merely with its like and are then wronged again: God is pardoning and most forgiving. So it will be, because God makes night pass into day, and day into night, and He is all hearing and all seeing. So it will be, because it is God alone who is the Truth, and whatever else they invoke is sheer falsehood: it is God who is the Most High, the Most Great.

Have you [Prophet] not considered how God sends water down from the sky and the next morning the earth

becomes green? God is truly most subtle, all aware; everything in the heavens and earth belongs to Him; God alone is
self-sufficient, worthy of all praise. Have you not considered
how God has made everything on the earth of service to you?
That ships sail the sea at His command? That He keeps the
heavens from falling down on the earth without His permission? God is most compassionate and most merciful to
mankind—it is He who gave you [people] life, will cause you
to die, then will give you life again—but man is ungrateful.

We have appointed acts of devotion for every community to observe, so do not let them argue with you [Prophet]
about this matter. Call them to your Lord—you are on the
right path—and if they argue with you, say, "God is well
aware of what you are doing." On the Day of Resurrection,
God will judge between you regarding your differences. Are
you [Prophet] not aware that God knows all that is in the
heavens and earth? All this is written in a Record; this is easy
for God.

Yet beside God they serve that for which He has sent no
authority and of which they have no knowledge: the evildoers will have no one to help them. [Prophet], you can see
the hostility on the faces of the disbelievers when Our messages are recited clearly to them: it is almost as if they are
going to attack those who recite Our messages to them. Say,
"'Shall I tell you what is far worse than what you feel now?
The Fire that God has promised the disbelievers! What a dismal end!" People, here is an illustration, so listen carefully:
those you call on beside God could not, even if they com-
bined all their forces, create a fly, and if a fly took something
away from them, they would not be able to retrieve it. How
feeble are the petitioners and how feeble are those they peti-

tion! They have no grasp of God's true measure: God is truly most strong and mighty.

God chooses messengers from among the angels and from among men. God is all hearing, all seeing: He knows what lies before and behind them. All matters return to Him. Believers, bow down, prostrate yourselves, worship your Lord, and do good so that you may succeed. Strive hard for God as is His due: He has chosen you and placed no hardship in your religion, the faith of your forefather Abraham. God has called you Muslims—both in the past and in this [message]—so that the Messenger can bear witness about you and so that you can bear witness about other people. So keep up the prayer, give the prescribed alms, and seek refuge in God: He is your protector—an excellent protector and an excellent helper.

Excerpts from *The Faith and Practice of Al-Ghāzāli*

by W. Montgomery Watt

Next I considered the circumstances of my life, and realized that I was caught in a veritable thicket of attachments. I also considered my activities, of which the best was my teaching and lecturing, and realized that in them I was dealing with sciences that were unimportant and contributed nothing to the attainment of eternal life.

After that I examined my motive in my work of teaching, and realized that it was not a pure desire for the things of God, but that the impulse moving me was the desire for an influential position and public recognition. I saw for certain that I was on the brink of a crumbling bank of sand and in imminent danger of hell-fire unless I set about to mend my ways.

I reflected on this continuously for a time, while the choice still remained open to me. One day I would form the resolution to quit **Baghdad** and get rid of these adverse circumstances; the next day I would abandon my resolution. I put one foot forward and drew the other back. If in the morning I had a genuine longing to seek eternal life, by the evening the attack of a whole host of desires had reduced it to impotence. Worldly desires were striving to keep me by their chains just where I was, while the voice of faith was calling, "To the road! to the road! What is left of life is but little and the journey before you is long. All that keeps you busy, both intellectually and practically, is but hypocrisy and delusion. If you do not prepare now for eternal life, when will you prepare? If you do not now sever these attachments, when will you sever

Next I considered
Al-Ghāzāli has previously explained that he had spent some time studying books on Sufism and that he had already reached some preliminary conclusions about its merit and meaning for his life.

Baghdad
Al-Ghāzāli's residence at this point in his narrative, Baghdad was for centuries a primary center of Islamic culture and learning.

them?" On hearing that, the impulse would be stirred and the resolution made to take to flight. . . .

In due course I entered **Damascus,** and there I remained for nearly two years with no other occupation than the cultivation of retirement and solitude, together with religious and ascetic exercises, as I busied myself purifying my soul, improving my character and cleansing my heart for the constant recollection of God most high, as I had learnt from my study of mysticism. I used to go into retreat for a period in the mosque of Damascus, going up the minaret of the mosque for the whole day and shutting myself in so as to be alone.

At length I made my way from Damascus to the **Holy House** (that is, Jerusalem). There I used to enter into the precinct of the **Rock** every day and shut myself in.

Next there arose in me a prompting to fulfil the duty of the Pilgrimage, gain the blessings of Mecca and **Medina,** and perform the visitation of

Damascus
city in modern-day Syria that for centuries, like Baghdad, was a major Islamic center

Holy House
the Dome of the Rock, one of Islam's most sacred shrines

Rock
refers to the place where Muslims believe the Prophet Muhammad ascended into Heaven on his Night Journey to Heaven

Medina
Originally named Yathrib, Medina is the Arabian city in which Muhammad first established the Islamic community.

the Messenger of God most high (peace be upon him), after first performing the visitation of al-Khalīl, the Friend of God (God bless him). I therefore made the journey to the Hijaz. Before long, however, various concerns, together with the entreaties of my children, drew me back to my home (country); and so I came to it again, though at one time no one had seemed less likely than myself to return to it. Here, too, I sought retirement, still longing for solitude and the purification of the heart for the recollection (of God). The events of the interval, the anxieties about my family, and the necessities of my livelihood altered the aspect of my purpose and impaired the quality of my solitude, for I experienced pure ecstasy only occasionally, although I did not cease to hope for that; obstacles would hold me back, yet I always returned to it.

I continued at this stage for the space of ten years, and during these periods of solitude there were revealed to me things innumerable and unfathomable. This much I shall say about that in order that others may be helped: I learnt with certainty that it is above all the mystics who walk on the road of God; their life is the best life, their method the soundest method, their character the purest character; indeed, were the intellect of the intellectuals and the learning of the learned and the scholarship of the scholars, who are versed in the profundities of revealed truth, brought together in the attempt to improve the life and character of the mystics, they would find no way of doing so; for to the mystics all movement and all rest, whether external or internal, brings illumination from the light of the lamp of prophetic revelation; and behind the light of prophetic revelation there is no other light on the face of the earth from which illumination may be received.

In general, then, how is a mystic "way" *(tariqah)* described? The purity which is the first condition of it (sc. as bodily purity is the prior condition of formal Worship for Muslims) is the purification of the heart completely from what is other than God most high; the key to it, which corresponds to the opening act of adoration in prayer, is the sinking of the heart completely in the recollection of God; and the end of it is complete absorption *(fanā')* in God. At least this is its end relatively to those first steps which almost come within the sphere of choice and personal responsibility; but in reality in the actual mystic "way" it is the first step, what comes before it being, as it were, the antechamber for those who are journeying towards it.

With this first stage of the "way" there begin the revelations and visions. The mystics in their waking state now behold angels and the spirits of the prophets; they hear these speaking to them and are instructed by them. Later, a higher state is reached; instead of beholding forms and figures, they come to stages in the "way" which it is hard to describe in language; if a man attempts to express these, his words inevitably contain what is clearly erroneous.

The Tagouris: One Family's Story

By Phyllis McIntosh

The Tagouris of La Plata, a small town in southern Maryland near Washington, D.C., are in many ways a typical American family. Father is a pathologist at the local hospital and serves as deputy medical examiner for Charles County. Mother is pursuing a Master's degree in counseling at Loyola College of Baltimore and hopes to become a licensed therapist in a school or in private practice. Like most suburban parents, they spend a lot of time on the road, ferrying their three children, ages 8, 5, and 3, to school and to dance classes, gymnastics, and Girl Scouts.

The Tagouris are also devout Muslims, and their faith is central to their busy lives. Despite his fast-paced job at the hospital, Dr. Yahia Tagouri drives to a nearby mosque at least once a day to make prayers, sometimes taking the children with him. For the other daily prayers, he retreats to his office. Most of his co-workers are non-Muslims, he says, but "when people see that my door is closed, they know it is **prayer time,** and they respect that." His wife, Salwa Omeish, who commutes about 180 miles round-trip to attend college classes, prays at home before and after school.

> **prayer time**
> early morning, noon, midafternoon, sunset, and evening

Deciding to Wear the Hijab

Unlike many Muslim girls in the United States today, who wear the **hijab** in high school, Salwa did not cover until several years ago. Wearing the hijab "was something in the back of my mind that I wanted to do," she says. "The main reason I wear it now is because God asks us to do it. It's a form of submission to

> **hijab**
> Arabic term for the head covering traditionally worn by Muslim women

God and not submitting to what society says we should look like."

Daughters Noor, a fourth-grader, and Yuser, just starting kindergarten, attended Christian preschools and now go to a public elementary school where virtually all the students are non-Muslim. There is no objection from teachers or school administrators when the girls stay home from school on Muslim holidays. And Noor's teacher welcomed Salwa into the classroom to decorate a "Happy Eid" bulletin board in observance of the Muslim holiday, which for the past several years has fallen around the same time as Christmas.

Although most of her children's young classmates now seem oblivious to religious differences, Salwa acknowledges that it may be more difficult for her children during the teen-age years than it was for her growing up in the Washington area. "We do worry, but we're strong in our faith," she says. "When we see differences, it doesn't bother us. We say, 'O.K., we don't do that and it's fine.'"

Because the local mosque, with only about 40 families, is too small to support religious classes, the Tagouri children spend the weekend with their grandparents or carpool with friends an hour in order to attend Islamic classes in northern Virginia. Noor, who at age 8 is learning to make her daily prayers, also receives religious instruction from a neighbor once or twice a week.

Will Noor and Yuser wear the hijab? The Tagouris stress that it will be strictly their daughters' decision. "You cannot force these things," Salwa says. "I could force them to put it on here, and they could go to school and take it off. We teach them that whatever they do in front of us or behind our backs, God is watching." "Once you teach them to see

God in everything they do and keep God in their hearts, then their faith will be strong, and they will want to obey God and his orders, whether it's praying, fasting, giving charity, or doing a good job in their work," adds Yahia. "And if they get to that point they will probably want to wear the hijab."

Teaching Islam by Example

Even though the Tagouris have spent their married life so far in less cosmopolitan areas of the United States, they say they have not been targets of religious intolerance. They believe strongly in spreading the message of their faith through example. "I don't talk about Islam that much," Yahia says, "but I try to show people what Islam should be by the way I live my life. Once they start to know me, they respect me for the man I am."

What does anger the Tagouris, however, is the frequent use of phrases like "Muslim militant" and "Muslim terrorist" in the media. Salwa points out that there have been native-born American terrorists like Timothy McVeigh, who bombed a federal building in Oklahoma City in 1995, killing 168, or the so-called Unabomber, who was responsible for a series of mail bombings. The press, she says, does not refer to these politically motivated murderers as a "Christian militant" or a "Christian bomber."

"To see Islam portrayed like this is hurtful," she says. "Islam comes from the word for peace. When we come into the house, instead of saying 'Hi' to each other, we say 'Peace be upon you.' Islam is all about peace, but too many people don't get that."

For Reflection

1. How does sura 22 portray the nature and attributes of God? What similarities do you see between the Islamic, Jewish, and Christian understandings of God?

2. Describe the Qur'an's literary style. What similarities does it share with other sacred texts, or sections from sacred texts, with which you are familiar?

3. Based on al-Ghāzāli's account, describe Sufism as he came to know and experience it.

4. "The main reason I wear it now is because God asks us to do it. It's a form of submission to God and not submitting to what society says we should look like." Based on your understanding of Islamic tradition, what is the meaning of submission that Salwa is referring to in this quote?

5. What incidents or attitudes have you witnessed that might make it difficult for Muslims in America to remain faithful to their religion?

Chapter 12

A World of Perspectives

A book on world religions inevitably poses challenges of categorization. Which traditions are to be included as world religions, and which are to be omitted? What about the many religions that are either relatively small in number of adherents or too new to have become established as traditions? Another challenge involves determining what counts as religion. In this chapter we give voice to an array of perspectives that have not found their way into the preceding chapters.

Jainism, with only about four million followers, the great majority of whom live in India, is a relatively small tradition, but it is ancient, with roots extending back at least to the eighth century BC. The central Jain doctrine of *ahimsa*, or nonviolence, is expressed through various practices of asceticism, or self-denial. To shed light on the remarkable extent to which Jain ascetics have traditionally gone in their pursuit of *ahimsa*, we include here a scriptural description of *sallekhana*, a form of self-starvation. While not commonly practiced, *sallekhana* illustrates the highest ideals of *ahimsa*.

Baha'i is a widespread religion that teaches that all the founders of the world's religious traditions have been God's divine messengers, or prophets. Baha'i's sacred text, *Kitab-i-aqdas*, is believed to contain the most recent revelations of the divine will, having been written by Baha Allah, who in 1863 proclaimed himself a prophet and founded the religion. As the excerpt here shows, Baha'i theology understands the one God to be deeply concerned about the moral quality of human beings.

Joseph Smith Jr. (1805–1844) founded in western New York the religious movement commonly known as Mormonism. Our excerpt comes from a section of Smith's *History of the Church of Jesus Christ of Latter-day Saints* and sets forth his account of his discovering the golden plates that he was to translate into the *Book of Mormon*.

Jehovah's Witnesses is another relatively new religion to have been founded in the United States. Charles Taze Russell (1852–1916) predicted, based on Bible chronology, that the world would be cleansed of wickedness by 1914. Russell also first published, in 1879, *The Watchtower*, a magazine (currently published semimonthly in more than 169 languages) that offers the perspectives of Jehovah's Witnesses. Our excerpt is drawn from a 2007 edition of *The Watchtower*.

Depending on how one defines religion, such worldviews as nationalism and secular humanism can be categorized as religious perspectives. Here we include a famous passage from one of the greatest influences on secular humanism, the German philosopher Friedrich Nietzsche. His famous statement "God is dead," rather than being simply a straightforward assertion of atheism, challenges the reader to try to make sense of a world that no longer depends on traditional religious authority for its moral compass.

Recognized by many as the religious perspective of Hollywood stars like Tom Cruise and John Travolta, Scientology offers a system of spiritual orientation that draws upon distinctively modern techniques. The movement's founder, L. Ron Hubbard, in 1950 famously set forth his understanding of these techniques in *Dianetics*, from which our excerpt is drawn.

Many modern religious movements focus on the power of nature. In our final excerpt, the well-known author and activist Starhawk describes one such movement, the Old Religion of the Goddess, or witchcraft.

This sample of perspectives hardly scratches the surface, in light of the vast array of religious traditions, ancient and modern, around the globe. But by exploring these seven perspectives, we can work toward expanding our range of vision to understand more clearly the entire vista of the world's religious landscape.

Jainism: Excerpt from the *Ācāraṅga Sutra*, 1.7, 6, on sallekhana (self-starvation)

monk

Only a small minority of Jains choose to be monks (or nuns, if the given sect permits it); regulations and expectations regarding asceticism are much more demanding for monks than for the laity.

If a **monk** feels sick, and is unable duly to mortify the flesh, he should regularly diminish his food. Mindful of his body, immovable as a beam, the monk should strive to waste his body away. He should enter a village or town . . . and beg for straw. Then he should take it and go to an out-of-the-way place. He should carefully inspect and sweep the ground, so that there are no eggs, living beings, sprouts, dew, water, ants, mildew, drops of water, mud, or cobwebs left on it. Thereupon he carries out the final fast. . . . Speaking the truth, the **saint who has crossed the stream of transmigration,** doing away with all hesitation, knowing

> **saint who has crossed the stream of transmigration**
> one who has attained *kevala,* the Jain term for perfect enlightenment, thus stepping off the wheel of rebirth (*samsāra,* the same term used by Hindus, Buddhists, and Sikhs)

all things but himself unknown, leaves his frail body. Overcoming manifold hardships and troubles, with trust in his religion he performs this terrible penance. Thus in due time he puts an end to his existence. This is done by those who have no delusions. This is good; this is joyful and proper; this leads to salvation; this should be followed.

Baha'i: Excerpt from the *Kitab-i-Aqdas*

IN THE NAME OF HIM WHO
IS THE SUPREME RULER
OVER ALL THAT HATH BEEN
AND ALL THAT IS TO BE

1
The first duty prescribed by God for His servants is the recognition of Him Who is the Dayspring of His Revelation and the Fountain of His laws, Who representeth the Godhead in

both the Kingdom of His Cause and the world of creation. Whoso achieveth this duty hath attained unto all good; and whoso is deprived thereof hath gone astray, though he be the author of every righteous deed. It behoveth every one who reacheth this most sublime station, this summit of transcendent glory, to observe every ordinance of Him Who is the Desire of the world. These twin duties are inseparable. Neither is acceptable without the other. Thus hath it been decreed by Him Who is the Source of Divine inspiration.

39

The peoples of the world are fast asleep. Were they to wake from their slumber, they would hasten with eagerness unto God, the All-Knowing, the All-Wise. They would cast away everything they possess, be it all the treasures of the earth, that their Lord may remember them to the extent of addressing to them but one word. Such is the instruction given you by Him Who holdeth the knowledge of things hidden, in a Tablet which the eye of creation hath not seen, and which is revealed to none except His own Self, the omnipotent Protector of all worlds. So bewildered are they in the drunkenness of their evil desires, that they are powerless to recognize the Lord of all being, Whose voice calleth aloud from every direction: "There is none other God but Me, the Mighty, the All-Wise."

40

Say: Rejoice not in the things ye possess; tonight they are yours, tomorrow others will possess them. Thus warneth you He Who is the All-Knowing, the All-Informed. Say: Can ye claim that what ye own is lasting or secure? Nay! By Myself, the All-Merciful, ye cannot, if ye be of them who judge fairly. The days of your life flee away as a breath of wind, and all your pomp and glory shall be folded up as were the pomp and glory of those gone before you. Reflect, O people!

What hath become of your bygone days, your lost centuries? Happy the days that have been consecrated to the remembrance of God, and blessed the hours which have been spent in praise of Him Who is the All-Wise. By My life! Neither the pomp of the mighty, nor the wealth of the rich, nor even the ascendancy of the ungodly will endure. All will perish, at a word from Him. He, verily, is the All-Powerful, the All-Compelling, the Almighty. What advantage is there in the earthly things which men possess? That which shall profit them, they have utterly neglected. Erelong, they will awake from their slumber, and find themselves unable to obtain that which hath escaped them in the days of their Lord, the Almighty, the All-Praised. Did they but know it, they would renounce their all, that their names may be mentioned before His throne. They, verily, are accounted among the dead.

Mormonism: Excerpt from "Joseph Smith—History: Extracts from *The History of Joseph Smith, the Prophet*"

1 Owing to the many reports which have been put in circulation by evil-disposed and designing persons, in relation to the rise and progress of the **Church of Jesus Christ of Latter-day Saints,** all of which have been designed by the authors thereof to militate against its character as a Church and its

Church of Jesus Christ of Latter-day Saints

Headquartered in Salt Lake City, this is the largest of a number of Mormon organizations that consider Joseph Smith Jr. to be their founder.

progress in the world—I have been induced to write this history, to disabuse the public mind, and put all inquirers after truth in possession of the facts, as they have transpired, in relation both to myself and the Church, so far as I have such facts in my possession.

2 In this history I shall present the various events in relation to this Church, in truth and righteousness, as they have transpired, or as they at present exist, being now [1838] the eighth year since the organization of the said Church. . . .

27 I continued to pursue my common vocations in life until the twenty-first of September, one thousand eight hundred and twenty-three, all the time suffering severe persecution at the hands of all classes of men, both religious and irreligious, because I continued to affirm that I had seen a vision.

28 During the space of time which intervened between the time I had the vision and the year eighteen hundred and twenty-three—having been forbidden to join any of the religious sects of the day, and being of very tender years, and persecuted by those who ought to have been my friends and to have treated me kindly, and if they supposed me to be deluded to have endeavored in a proper and affectionate manner to have reclaimed me—I was left to all kinds of temptations; and, mingling with all kinds of society, I frequently fell into many foolish errors, and displayed the weakness of youth, and the foibles of human nature; which, I am sorry to say, led me into divers temptations, offensive in

the sight of God. In making this confession, no one need suppose me guilty of any great or malignant sins. A disposition to commit such was never in my nature. But I was guilty of levity, and sometimes associated with jovial company, etc., not consistent with that character which ought to be maintained by one who was called of God as I had been. But this will not seem very strange to any one who recollects my youth, and is acquainted with my native cheery temperament.

29 In consequence of these things, I often felt condemned for my weakness and imperfections; when, on the evening of the above-mentioned twenty-first of September, after I had retired to my bed for the night, I betook myself to prayer and supplication to Almighty God for forgiveness of all my sins and follies, and also for a manifestation to me, that I might know of my state and standing before him; for I had full confidence in obtaining a divine manifestation, as I previously had one.

30 While I was thus in the act of calling upon God, I discovered a light appearing in my room, which continued to increase until the room was lighter than at noonday, when immediately a personage appeared at my bedside, standing in the air, for his feet did not touch the floor.

31 He had on a loose robe of most exquisite whiteness. It was a whiteness beyond anything earthly I had ever seen; nor do I believe that any earthly thing could be made to appear so exceedingly white and brilliant. His hands were naked, and his arms also, a little above the wrist; so, also, were his feet naked, as were his legs, a little above the ankles. His head and neck were also bare. I could discover that he had no other clothing on but this robe, as it was open, so that I could see into his bosom.

Moroni
Here appearing as a resurrected person, in his earthly life the son of Mormon, who is believed to have been a prophet who inscribed the golden plates that centuries later Joseph Smith Jr. rediscovered and translated into the Book of Mormon; Moroni is believed to have sent the plates up to God to be hidden away about AD 421 until the "latter days."

former inhabitants of this continent
Mormons believe that ancient Israelites who had set sail about 600 BC established a civilization in North America, where the resurrected Christ visited them.

the Savior
Christ

32 Not only was his robe exceedingly white, but his whole person was glorious beyond description, and his countenance truly like lightning. The room was exceedingly light, but not so very bright as immediately around his person. When I first looked upon him, I was afraid; but the fear soon left me.

33 He called me by name, and said unto me that he was a messenger sent from the presence of God to me, and that his name was **Moroni;** that God had a work for me to do; and that my name should be had for good and evil among all nations, kindreds, and tongues, or that it should be both good and evil spoken of among all people.

34 He said there was a book deposited, written upon gold plates, giving an account of the **former inhabitants of this continent,** and the source from whence they sprang. He also said that the fulness of the everlasting Gospel was

contained in it, as delivered by **the Savior** to the ancient inhabitants . . .

Jehovah's Witnesses: Excerpt from *Awake!:* "Where Is This World Headed?"

The Bible foretold the present moral breakdown long in advance and described it this way: "*In the last days* critical times hard to deal with will be here. For men will be lovers of themselves, lovers of money, . . . disobedient to parents, unthankful, disloyal, having no natural affection, . . . fierce, without love of goodness, betrayers, headstrong, puffed up with pride, lovers of pleasures rather than lovers of God, having a form of godly devotion but proving false to its power."—2 Timothy 3:1–5.

You may agree that this Bible prophecy is an accurate description of the world today. Yet, it was recorded nearly 2,000 years ago! The prophecy is introduced with the words: "*In the last days*." What does that expression, "the last days," mean?

"The Last Days" of What?

"The last days" has become a very common expression. In the English language alone, it has been part of the title of hundreds of books. Consider, for example, the recent book *The Last Days of Innocence—America at War, 1917–1918*. The prologue makes clear that when using the term "the last days," the book refers to a specific time, one in which there has been a tremendous decay in morals.

"In 1914," the prologue explains, "the country was changing more rapidly than at any time in its history." Indeed, the year 1914 marked a plunge into war worldwide, which had not been experienced before. The book says: "This was total war, the conflict not of army against army but nation against nation." This war, as we will see, occurred at the beginning of what the Bible terms "the last days."

That this world would experience before its actual end a specific time called "the last days" is a teaching of the Bible. The Bible, in fact, says that a world once existed that has already passed away, or ended, explaining: "The world of that time suffered destruction when it was deluged with water." What time was that, and what was the world that ended? It was the ancient "world of ungodly people" that existed in the days of the man Noah. Similarly, today's world will end. Yet, those who serve God will survive the end, as did Noah and his family.—2 Peter 2:5; 3:6; Genesis 7:21–24; 1 John 2:17.

What Jesus Said About the End

Jesus Christ also spoke of "the days of Noah," when "the flood came and swept them all away." He compared conditions that existed before the Flood—just prior to the end of that world—with those that would prevail during the time that he identified as "the conclusion of the system of things." (Matthew 24:3, 37–39) Other Bible translations use the expression "the end of the world" or "the end of the age."— *The Jerusalem Bible, The New English Bible,* and the *New International Version.*

Jesus foretold what life would be like on earth just before the world's end. Regarding war, he said: "Nation will rise against nation and kingdom against kingdom." Historians have noted that this occurred beginning in 1914. Thus, the prologue of the aforementioned book spoke of 1914 as marking the beginning of "total war, . . . not of army against army but nation against nation."

In his prophecy, Jesus added: "There will be food shortages and earthquakes in one place after another. All these things are a beginning of pangs of distress." He went on to say that among other things there would be an *increasing of lawlessness*." (Matthew 24:7–14) Surely we have seen this occur in our day. Today's moral breakdown is so severe that it is fulfilling Bible prophecy!

Secular Humanism: Excerpt from *The Gay Science:* "Parable of the Madman," by Friedrich Nietzsche

Have you not heard of that madman who lit a lantern in the bright morning hours, ran to the market place, and cried incessantly: "I seek God! I seek God!"—As many of those who did not believe in God were standing around just then, he provoked much laughter. Has he got lost? asked one. Did he lose his way like a child? asked another. Or is he hiding? Is he afraid of us? Has he gone on a voyage? emigrated?—Thus they yelled and laughed.

The madman jumped into their midst and pierced them with his eyes. "Whither is God?" he cried; "I will tell you.

We have killed him—you and I. All of us are his murderers. But how did we do this? How could we drink up the sea? Who gave us the sponge to wipe away the entire horizon? What were we doing when we unchained this earth from its sun? Whither is it moving now? Whither are we moving? Away from all suns? Are we not plunging continually? Backward, sideward, forward, in all directions? Is there still any up or down? Are we not straying as through an infinite nothing? Do we not feel the breath of empty space? Has it not become colder? Is not night continually closing in on us? Do we not need to light lanterns in the morning? Do we hear nothing as yet of the noise of the gravediggers who are burying God? Do we smell nothing as yet of the divine decomposition? Gods, too, decompose. God is dead. God remains dead. And we have killed him.

"How shall we comfort ourselves, the murderers of all murderers? What was holiest and mightiest of all that the world has yet owned has bled to death under our knives: who will wipe this blood off us? What water is there for us to clean ourselves? What festivals of atonement, what sacred games shall we have to invent? Is not the greatness of this deed too great for us? Must we ourselves not become gods simply to appear worthy of it? There has never been a greater deed; and whoever is born after us—for the sake of this deed he will belong to a higher history than all history hitherto."

Here the madman fell silent and looked again at his listeners; and they, too, were silent and stared at him in astonishment. At last he threw his lantern on the ground, and it broke into pieces and went out. "I have come too early," he said then; "my time is not yet. This tremendous event is still on its way, still wandering; it has not yet reached the ears of men. Lightning and thunder require time; the light of the stars requires time; deeds, though done, still require time to be seen and heard. This deed is still more distant from them than the most distant stars—*and yet they have done it themselves.*"

It has been related further that on the same day the madman forced his way into several churches and there struck up his **requiem aeternam deo.** Led out and called to account, he is said always to have replied nothing but "What after all are these churches now if they are not the tombs and sepulchers of God?"

> **requiem aeternam deo**
> Latin, "to God eternal rest"

Scientology: Excerpt from *Dianetics: The Modern Science of Mental Health*

by L. Ron Hubbard

Dianetically, the optimum individual is called the clear. One will hear much of that word, both as a noun and a verb, in this volume, so it is well to spend time here at the outset setting forth exactly what can be called a clear, the goal of Dianetic therapy.

A *clear* can be tested for any and all psychoses, neuroses, compulsions and repressions (all aberrations) and can be examined for any autogenetic (self-generated) diseases referred to as psychosomatic ills. These tests confirm the *clear* to be entirely without such ills or aberrations. Additional tests of his intelligence indicate it to be high above the current norm. Observation of his activity demonstrates that he pursues existence with vigor and satisfaction.

Further, these results can be obtained on a comparative basis. A neurotic individual, possessed also of psychosomatic ills, can be tested for those aberrations and illnesses, demonstrating that they exist. He can then be given Dianetic therapy to the end of clearing these neuroses and ills. Finally, he can be examined, with the above results. This, in passing, is an experiment which has been performed many times with invariable results. It is a matter of laboratory test that all individuals who have organically complete nervous systems respond in this fashion to Dianetic clearing.

Further, the clear possesses attributes, fundamental and inherent but not always available in an uncleared state, which have not been suspected of man and are not included in past discussions of his abilities and behavior.

First there is the matter of perceptions. Even so-called normal people do not always see in full color, hear in full tone or sense at the optimum with their organs of smell, taste, tactile and organic sensation.

These are the main lines of communication to the finite world which most people recognize as reality. It is an interesting commentary that while past observers felt that the facing of reality was an absolute necessity if the aberrated individual wished to be sane, no definition of how this was to be done was set forth. To face reality in the present, one would certainly have to be able to sense it along those channels of communication most commonly used by man in his affairs.

The Old Religion of the Goddess: Excerpt from *Dreaming the Dark: Magic, Sex and Politics*

by Starhawk

The Old Religion—call it Witchcraft, **Wicca,** the Craft, or with a slightly broader definition, **Paganism or Neo-Paganism**—is both old and newly invented. Its roots go back to the pre-Judeo-Christian tribal religions of the West, and it is akin in spirit, form, and practice to Native American and African religions. Its myths and symbols draw from the woman-valuing, matristic, Goddess-centered cultures that underlie the beginnings of civilization. It is not a religion with a dogma, a doctrine, or a sacred book; it is a religion of experience, of ritual, of practices that change consciousness

Wicca
(Old English, "sorcerer") a subcategory of Neo-paganism that features goddess-worship and various rituals practiced by groups called covens, usually performed secretly

Paganism or Neo-Paganism
From the Latin *paganus,* "inhabitant of the countryside," *paganism* generally refers to a broad category of non-Jewish and non-Christian religions of ancient Europe and western Asia; the similarly broad modern category Neo-Paganism (sometimes simply "Paganism") draws inspiration, ideas, and practices from these ancient traditions.

and awaken power-from-within. Beneath all, it is a religion of connection with the Goddess, who is immanent in nature, in human beings, in relationships. Because the Goddess is here, She is eternally inspirational. And so Witchcraft is eternally reinvented, changing, growing, alive.

Long after city dwellers had converted to Christianity, the Witches were the wise women and cunning men of the country villages. They were the herbalists, the healers, the counselors in times of trouble. Their seasonal celebrations established the bond between individuals, the community as a whole, and the land and its resources. That bond, that deep connection, was the source of life—human, plant, animal, and spiritual. Without it, nothing could grow. From the power within that relationship came the ability to heal, to divine the future, to build, to create, to make songs, to birth children, to build culture. The bond was erotic, sensual, carnal, because the activities of the flesh were not separate from the spirit immanent in life.

The history of patriarchal civilization could be read as a cumulative effort to break that bond, to drive a wedge between spirit and flesh, culture and nature, man and woman. One of the major battles in that long war of conquest was fought in the sixteenth and seventeenth centuries, when the persecutions of the Witches shattered the peasants' connection with the land, drove women out of the work of healing, and imposed the mechanist view of the world as a dead machine. That rupture underlies the entwined oppressions of race, sex, class, and ecological destruction.

The Craft survived, however—secretly, silently, underground, in small groups called covens whose members were related by blood or deep trust. Its reemergence in this century is linked to a growing realization among many strata of people that the dead world of mechanism, the world of domination, cannot sustain our inner lives, nor our lives in community with each other, nor the life of the planet. The rebirth of earth religion is a part of a broad movement that challenges domination—that seeks to connect with the root, the heart, the source of life by changing our present relationships.

For Reflection

1. How does the Jain practice of *sallekhana* follow the principle of *ahimsa,* or nonviolence? What are the results of this practice, and why do you think Jainism regards them as good?

2. Review sura 22 of the Qur'an (in chapter 11). Compare the portrayal of God there with that of Baha'i, based on the excerpt from Kitab-i-Aqdas.

3. Summarize Joseph Smith Jr.'s account of his encounter with Moroni. Based on this account, describe Smith's role in the founding of the Mormon religion.

4. Identify the main focus of the excerpt from *The Watchtower.* How does the article incorporate references to modern historical events to fortify its arguments?

5. "We have killed him—you and I." In what ways does this statement by Friedrich Nietzsche differ or go beyond his more famous statement a few sentences later, "God is dead"? What do you think Nietzsche intends by having his madman state, near the end of this parable, "I have come too early"?

6. Describe a person who, in the language of Dianetics, is a clear. Based on this excerpt, to what extent does Scientology seem to strive to apply the aims and methods of science?

7. Drawing upon the excerpt from Starhawk's *Dreaming the Dark,* give a summary description of the Old Religion. What do you find notable or surprising about her description of this form of witchcraft?

Appendix

General Interest

Earhart, H. Byron, ed. *Religious Traditions of the World: A Journey Through Africa, Mesoamerica, North America, Judaism, Christianity, Islam, Hinduism, Buddhism, China, and Japan.* San Francisco: HarperSanFrancisco, 1993.

Eastman, Roger, ed. *The Ways of Religion: An Introduction to the Major Traditions.* 3rd ed. New York: Oxford University Press, 1999.

Eliade, Mircea, ed. *The Encyclopedia of Religion.* 16 vols. New York: Macmillan, 1987.

Fisher, Mary Pat. *Living Religions.* 7th ed. Upper Saddle River, NJ: Prentice-Hall, 2007.

Noss, David S., and Blake R. Grangaard. *A History of the World's Religions.* 12th ed. New York: Macmillan, 2007.

Sharma, Arvind, ed. *Our Religions.* San Francisco: HarperSanFrancisco, 1993.

Smart, Ninian. *The World's Religions: Old Traditions and Modern Transformations.* 2nd ed. Cambridge, England: Cambridge University Press, 1998.

———. *Worldviews: Crosscultural Explorations of Human Beliefs.* 3rd ed. New York: Scribner, 1999.

Smart, Ninian, and Richard D. Hecht, eds. *Sacred Texts of the World: A Universal Anthology.* New York: Crossroad Publishing, 1982.

Smith, Huston. *The World's Religions*. San Francisco: HarperSan-Francisco, 1991.

Smith, Jonathan Z., ed. *The HarperCollins Dictionary of Religion*. San Francisco: HarperSanFrancisco, 1995.

Chapter 1: The Catholic Church and World Religions

Sherwin, Byron, and Harold Kasimow, eds. *John Paul II and Inter-religious Dialogue*. New York: Orbis, 1999.

Chapter 2: Primal Religious Traditions

Berndt, Ronald M. *Australian Aboriginal Religion*. Leiden, Netherlands: Brill Academic Publishers, 1974.

Drewal, Henry John. *Yoruba: Nine Centuries of African Art and Thought*. New York: Center for African Art, in association with H. N. Abrams, 1989.

Gill, Sam D. *Native American Religions: An Introduction*. The Religious Life of Man series. Belmont, CA: Wadsworth, 1982.

Hultkrantz, Ake. *The Religions of American Indians*. Berkeley, CA: University of California Press, 1979.

Lawson, E. Thomas. *Religions of Africa: Traditions in Transformation*. Prospect Heights, IL: Waveland, 1998.

Parrinder, Edward Geoffrey. *West African Religion: A Study of the Beliefs and Practices of Akan, Ewe, Yoruba, Ibo, and Kindred Peoples*. 2nd ed. London: Epworth Press, 1961.

Ray, Benjamin C. *African Religions: Symbol, Ritual, and Community*. 2nd ed. Upper Saddle River, NJ: Prentice-Hall, 1999.

Chapter 3: Hinduism

Basham, A. L. *The Wonder That Was India: A Survey of the Culture of the Indian Sub-Continent Before the Coming of the Muslims.* New York: Grove, 1954.

Ellsberg, Robert, ed. *Gandhi on Christianity.* Maryknoll, NY: Orbis, 1991.

Hopkins, Thomas J. *The Hindu Religious Tradition.* The Religious Life of Man series. Belmont, CA: Wadsworth, 1971.

Kinsley, David T. *Hinduism: A Cultural Perspective. 2nd ed.* Prentice-Hall Series in World Religions. Englewood Cliffs, NJ: Prentice-Hall, 1993.

Knipe, David M. *Hinduism: Experiments in the Sacred.* Prospect Heights, IL: Waveland, 1998.

Mascaro, Juan, trans. *The Upanishads.* New York: Penguin, 1965.

Miller, Barbara Stoler, trans. *The Bhagavad-Gita: Krishna's Counsel in Time of War.* New York: Bantam Books, 1986.

O'Flaherty, Wendy Doniger, trans. *The Rig Veda.* New York: Penguin, 1981.

Prabhavananda, Swami. *The Spiritual Heritage of India.* Hollywood, CA: Vedanta Press, 1963.

Prabhavananda, Swami, and Christopher Isherwood, trans. *The Song of God: Bhagavad-Gita.* Hollywood, CA: Vedanta Press, 1944.

Radhakrishnan, Sarvepalli, and Charles A. Moore, eds. *A Source Book in Indian Philosophy.* Princeton, NJ: Princeton University Press, 1957.

Renou, Louis, ed. *Hinduism.* New York: Braziller, 1962.

Zimmer, Heinrich. *The Philosophies of India.* Princeton, NJ: Princeton University Press, 1969.

Chapter 4: Buddhism

Aitken, Robert. *Taking the Path of Zen.* San Francisco: North Point, 1982.

Chan, Wing-tsit, trans. and comp. *A Source Book in Chinese Philosophy*. Princeton, NJ: Princeton University Press, 1963.

Ch'en, Kenneth K. S. *Buddhism in China*. Princeton, NJ: Princeton University Press, 1973.

Conze, Edward, trans. *Buddhist Scriptures*. New York: Penguin, 1959.

Gyatso, Tenzin. *Freedom in Exile: The Autobiography of the Dalai Lama*. San Francisco: HarperSanFrancisco, 1990.

Kapleau, Philip. *The Three Pillars of Zen*. New York: Anchor, 1989.

Radhakrishnan, Sarvepalli, and Charles A. Moore, eds. *A Source Book in Indian Philosophy*. Princeton, NJ: Princeton University Press, 1957.

Rahula, Walpola. *What the Buddha Taught*. Rev. ed. New York: Grove, 1974.

Robinson, Richard H., and Willard L. Johnson. *The Buddhist Religion: A Historical Introduction*. 4th ed. The Religious Life of Man series. Belmont, CA: Wadsworth, 1997.

Suzuki, D. T. *An Introduction to Zen Buddhism*. New York: Grove Press, 1964.

Suzuki, Shunryu. *Zen Mind, Beginner's Mind*. New York: Weatherhill, 1970.

Warren, Henry Clarke, trans. *Buddhism in Translation*. New York: Atheneum, 1962.

Chapter 5: Sikhism

Cole, W. Owen, and Piara Singh Sambhi. *The Sikhs: Their Religious Beliefs and Practices*. 2nd rev. ed. Brighton, United Kingdom: Sussex Academic Press, 1995.

McLeod, W. Hew. *Sikhism*. London: Penguin, 1997.

———, ed. and trans. *Textual Sources for the Study of Sikhism*. Totowa, NJ: Barnes & Noble Books, 1984.

Singh, Trilochan, Jodh Singh, Kapur Singh, Bawa Harishen Singh, and Khushwant Singh, trans. *The Sacred Writings of the Sikhs*. London: George Allen and Unwin, 1960.

Chapter 6: Confucianism

Chan, Wing-tsit, trans. and comp. *A Source Book in Chinese Philosophy*. Princeton, NJ: Princeton University Press, 1963.

Confucius. *Confucius: The Analects*. Trans. D. C. Lau. New York: Penguin, 1979.

Creel, H. G. *Chinese Thought: From Confucius to Mao Tse-Tung*. Chicago: University of Chicago Press, 1953.

———. *Confucius and the Chinese Way*. New York: Harper and Row, 1960.

Fingarette, Herbert. *Confucius: The Secular as Sacred*. New York: Harper and Row, 1972.

Thompson, Laurence G. *Chinese Religion: An Introduction*. 5th ed. The Religious Life of Man series. Belmont, CA: Wadsworth, 1995.

Chapter 7: Taoism

Chan, Wing-tsit, trans. and comp. *A Source Book in Chinese Philosophy*. Princeton, NJ: Princeton University Press, 1963.

Chuang Tzu. *Chuang Tzu: Basic Writings*. Trans. Burton Watson. New York: Columbia University Press, 1964.

———. *The Complete Works of Chuang Tzu*. Trans. Burton Watson. New York: Columbia University Press, 1968.

Kaltenmark, Max. *Lao Tzu and Taoism*. Trans. Roger Greaves. Stanford, CA: Stanford University Press, 1969.

Lao Tzu. *Tao Te Ching*. Trans. Gia-fu Feng and Jane English. New York: Knopf, 1974.

———. *The Way of Lao Tzu (Tao Te Ching)*. Trans. Wing-tsit Chan. Indianapolis: Bobbs-Merrill, 1963.

Thompson, Laurence G. *Chinese Religion: An Introduction*. 5th ed. The Religious Life of Man Series. Belmont, CA: Wadsworth, 1996.

Chapter 8: Shinto

Earhart, H. Byron. *Japanese Religion: Unity and Diversity*. 4th ed. The Religious Life of Man series. Belmont, CA: Wadsworth, 2003.

———, ed. *Religion in the Japanese Experience: Sources and Interpretations*. 2nd ed. The Religious Life of Man series. Belmont, CA: Wadsworth, 1997.

Tsunoda, Ryusaku, William Theodore de Bary, and Donald Keene, eds. *Sources of Japanese Tradition*. New York: Columbia University Press, 1958.

Chapter 9: Judaism

Danby, Herbert, ed. and trans. *The Mishnah*. Oxford, England: Oxford University Press, 1933.

Encyclopædia Judaica. 16 vols. New York: Macmillan, 1971.

Fishbane, Michael A. *Judaism: Revelation and Traditions*. San Francisco: Harper and Row, 1987.

Montefiore, C. G., and H. J. Lowe, eds. *A Rabbinic Anthology*. New York: Schocken, 1974.

Neusner, Jacob. *The Way of Torah: An Introduction to Judaism*. 7th ed. The Religious Life of Man series. Belmont, CA: Wadsworth, 2003.

———, ed. *The Life of Torah: Readings in the Jewish Religious Experience*. The Religious Life of Man series. Belmont, CA: Wadsworth, 1974.

Seltzer, Robert M. *Jewish People, Jewish Thought: The Jewish Experience in History*. New York: Macmillan, 1980.

Steinsaltz, Adin. *The Essential Talmud*. New York: Basic Books, 1976.

Tanakh: A New Translation of the Holy Scriptures According to the Traditional Hebrew Text. Philadelphia: Jewish Publication Society, 1985.

Chapter 10: Christianity

Augustine, Saint. *Confessions*. Trans. R. S. Pine-Coffin. New York: Penguin, 1961.

Brown, Peter. *Augustine of Hippo: A Biography*. Berkeley, CA: University of California Press, 1967.

Harris, Stephen. *The New Testament: A Student's Introduction*. 6th ed. New York: McGraw-Hill, 2008.

Johnson, Paul. *A History of Christianity*. New York: Atheneum, 1976.

Metzger, Bruce M., and Roland E. Murphy. *The New Oxford Annotated Bible with the Apocryphal/Deuterocanonical Books*. New Revised Standard Version. New York: Oxford University Press, 1991.

Reynolds, Stephen. *The Christian Religious Tradition*. The Religious Life of Man series. Belmont, CA: Wadsworth, 1977.

Chapter 11: Islam

Cragg, Kenneth. *The House of Islam*. The Religious Life of Man series. 3rd ed. Belmont, CA: Wadsworth, 1988.

Cragg, Kenneth, and R. Marston Speight. *Islam from Within: Anthology of a Religion*. The Religious Life of Man series. Belmont, CA: Wadsworth, 1980.

Denny, Frederick Mathewson. *An Introduction to Islam*. 3rd ed. New York: Macmillan, 2005.

Esposito, John L. *Islam: The Straight Path*. 3rd ed. New York: Oxford University Press, 2004.

Haddad, Yvonne Yazbeck, ed. *The Muslims of America*. New York: Oxford University Press, 1991.

Kritzeck, James, ed. *Anthology of Islamic Literature: From the Rise of Islam to Modern Times*. New York: Holt, Rinehart, and Winston, 1964.

Lings, Martin. *What Is Sufism?* New York: Routledge, Chapman, Hall, 1988.

Pickthall, Mohammed Marmaduke, trans. *The Meaning of the Glorious Koran*. New York: New American Library, 1953.

Rahman, Fazlur. *Islam*. 2nd ed. Chicago: University of Chicago Press, 1979.

Schimmel, Annemarie. *Mystical Dimensions of Islam*. Chapel Hill, NC: University of North Carolina Press, 1975.

Schuon, Frithjof. *Understanding Islam*. Chicago: Kazi Publications, 1996.

Chapter 12: A World of Perspectives

Book of Mormon: Another Testament of Jesus Christ. 1830. Reprint, Salt Lake City: Church of Jesus Christ of Latter-day Saints, 1981.

Dundas, Paul. *The Jains*. 2nd ed. London: Routledge, 2002.

Gaver, Jessyca Russell. *The Baha'i Faith: Dawn of a New Day*. New York: Hawthorn Books, 1967.

Jaini, Padmanabh S. *The Jaina Path of Purification*. Berkeley, CA: University of California Press, 1979.

Lewis, James R. *The Encyclopedic Sourcebook of New Age Religions*. Amherst, NY: Prometheus, 2004.

Melton, J. Gordon. *Encyclopedia of American Religions*. 7th ed. Detroit: Gale, 2002.

Starhawk. *The Spiral Dance: A Rebirth of the Ancient Religion of the Great Goddess*. San Francisco: Harper and Row, 1979.

Acknowledgments

The *Nostra Aetate* quotation on page 13 and the excerpt on pages 14–20 are from *Declaration on the Relation of the Church to Non-Christian Religions (Nostra Aetate)*, numbers 2 and 1–5, at *www.vatican.va/archive/hist_councils/ ii_vatican_council/documents/vat-ii_decl_19651028_nostra-aetate_en.html*, accessed September 6, 2008. Copyright © 1965 by Libreria Editrice Vaticana. Used with permission of Libreria Editrice Vaticana.

The excerpt in the section on pages 20–26 and the quotations on the back cover are from "Meeting with Representatives of Other Religions: Address of His Holiness Benedict XVI," at *www.vatican.va/holy_father/benedict_xvi/ speeches/2008/april/documents/hf_ben-xvi_spe_20080417_other-religions_ en.html*, accessed September 6, 2008. Copyright © 2008 by Libreria Editrice Vaticana. Used with permission of Libreria Editrice Vaticana.

The story "The Birth of the Butterflies" on pages 30–34 is from *Myths and Legends of the Australian Aboriginals*, by W. Ramsay Smith (London: George G. Harrap and Company; reprint: New York: Johnson Reprint Corporation, 1970), pages 59–62.

The excerpt on pages 34–35 is from *The Altar of My Soul: The Living Traditions of Santeria*, by Marta Moreno Vega (New York: Ballantine Publishing Group, a division of Random House), page 9. Copyright © 2000 by Marta Moreno Vega. Illustrations copyright © 2000 by Manuel Vega. Used with permission of the author and Ballantine Books, a division of Random House, Inc.

The excerpt on pages 36–40 is from *Lakota Woman*, by Mary Crow Dog and Richard Erdoes (New York: HarperCollins, 1991), pages 153–155. Translation copyright © 1990 by Mary Crow Dog and Richard Erdoes. Used with permission of Grove/Atlantic, Inc.

The excerpt on pages 43–54 is from *The Bhagavad-Gita: Krishna's Counsel in the Time of War*, translated by Barbara Stoler Miller (New York: Bantam Book, 1986), pages 29–46. English translation copyright © by Barbara Stoller Miller. Used with permission of Bantam Books, a division of Random House, Inc.

The excerpt on pages 55–58 is from *Philosophies of India*, by Heinrich Zimmer, edited by Joseph Campbell (New York: Meridian Books, 1956), pages 19–22. Copyright © 1951 by Bollingen Foundation, New York, 1979 renewed. Reprinted with permission of Princeton University Press.

The excerpt on pages 58–60 is from *All Men Are Brothers: Life and Thoughts of Mahatma Gandhi as Told in His Own Words*, compiled and edited by Krishna Kripalani (World Without War Publications, reprinted by arrangement

The excerpt on pages 136–139 is from *The Taoist Body*, by Kristofer Schipper, translated by Karen C. Duval (Berkeley, CA: University of California Press), pages 1–3. Copyright © 1993 by the Regents of the University of California. Used with permission of the University of California.

The excerpts on pages 143–147 and 147–153 are from *Sources of Japanese Tradition*, compiled by Ryusaku Tsunoda, Wm. Theodore de Bary, and Donald Keene (New York: Columbia University Press, 1958), pages 16–19 and 520–523. Copyright © 1958 by Columbia University Press. Used with permission of Columbia University Press.

The excerpt on pages 153–154 is from *Motoori Norinaga Zensh (Complete Works of Motoori Norinaga)*, by Motoori Norinaga (Tokyo, 1901), pages 150–152, as quoted in *The National Faith of Japan: A Study in Modern Shinto*, by D. C. Holtom (New York: Paragon Book Reprint Corp., 1965), pages 23–24.

The Scripture excerpts on pages 158–163 and 180–190 are from the New Revised Standard Version of the Bible, Catholic Edition. Copyright © 1993 and 1989 by the Division of Christian Education of the National Council of the Churches of Christ in the United States. Used with permission. All rights reserved.

The excerpt on pages 163–173 is from *Pirke Aboth: Sayings of the Fathers*, edited with translations and commentaries by Isaac Unterman (New York: Twayne Publishers, 1964), pages 65–68 and 72–73. Copyright © 1964 by Isaac Unterman.

The excerpt on pages 173–176 is from *The Family Markowitz*, by Allegra Goodman (New York: Farrar, Straus and Giroux, 1996), pages 193–197. Copyright © 1996 by Allegra Goodman. Used with permission.

The excerpt on pages 190–193 is from *Confessions*, by Saint Augustine; translated with an introduction by R. S. Pine-Coffin (London: Penguin Books, 1961) pages 177–179. Copyright © 1961 by R. S. Pine-Coffin. Used with permission of Penguin Books, Ltd.

The excerpt on pages 194–198 is from *Concluding Unscientific Postscript to Philosophical Fragments: Volume I: Text,* by Søren Kierkegaard; edited and translated by Howard V. Hong and Edna H. Hong (Princeton, NJ: Princeton University Press), pages 607–611. Copyright © 1992 by Princeton University Press. Reprinted with permission of Princeton University Press.

The excerpt on pages 201–209 is from *The Qur'an*, a new translation by M. A. S. Abdel Haleem (New York: Oxford University Press, 2004), pages 209–214. Copyright © 2004, 2005 by M. A. S. Abdel Haleem. Used with permission of Oxford University Press.

The excerpts on pages 209–213 is from *The Faith and Practice of Al-Ghāzāli,* by W. Montgomery Watt (London: George Allen and Unwin, Ltd., 1953), pages 56–57 and 59–61.

The excerpt on pages 213–216 is from "The Tagouris: One Family's Story," by Phyllis McIntosh, for the U.S. Department of State's Bureau of International

Information Programs, at *redir.aspx?C=7a26cf5042d14c54bb96237c7de03ec c&URL=http%3a%2f%2f209.85.173.132%2fsearch%3fq%3dcache%3ajinb 8CWo2YQJ%3abeijing.usembassy-china.org.cn%2fuploads%2fimages%2f2G UDXXd4ONttpxps8TETNA%2fmuslimlife_in_america.pdf%2bPhyllis%2bMcl ntosh%2band%2bTagouris%26hl%3den%26ct%3dclnk%26cd%3d3%26gl %3dus%234"http://209.85.173.132/search?q=cache:jinb8CWo2YQJ:beijing. usembassy-china.org.cn/uploads/images/2GUDXXd4ONttpxps8TETNA/muslim-life_in_america.pdf+Phyllis+McIntosh+and+Tagouris&hl=en&ct=clnk&cd=3&gl= us#4,* accessed October 27, 2008.

The excerpt on pages 220–221 from the *Ācārāṅga Sūtra* is quoted from *Sources of Indian Tradition,* second edition, volume 1, edited and revised by Ainslie T. Embree (New York: Columbia University Press, 1988), page 72. Copyright © 1988 by Columbia University Press.

The excerpt on pages 221–223 is from the *Kitab-i-Aqdas,* numbers 1, 39, and 40, respectively, at *www.sacred-texts.com/bhi/aqdas.htm,* accessed September 6, 2008. Copyright © 1994 by the Baha'i International Community. Used with permission of the Baha'i International Community.

The excerpt on pages 223–227 is from "Joseph Smith—History: Extracts from *The History of Joseph Smith, the Prophet,*" at *www.scriptures.lds.org/en/ js_h/1/27-34,* accessed September 6, 2008.

The excerpt on pages 227–229 is from "Where Is This World Headed?" in *Awake!,* companion publication of the *Watchtower,* April 2007, at *www. watchtower.org/e/200704/article_01.htm,* accessed September 6, 2008. Reprinted with permission of Watch Tower Bible and Tract Society of Pennsylvania.

The excerpt on pages 229–231 is from *The Gay Science:* "Parable of the Madman," by Friedrich Nietzsche, translated by Walter Kaufmann (New York: Random House, 1974), pages 181–182. Copyright © 1974 by Random House. Used with permission of Random House, Inc., and Walter Kaufmann Copyright Trust.

The excerpt on pages 231–232 is from *Dianetics: The Modern Science of Mental Health,* by L. Ron Hubbard (Los Angeles: Bridge Publications, 1985), pages 12–13. Copyright © 1985 by L. Ron Hubbard.

The excerpt on pages 233–235 is from *Dreaming the Dark: Magic, Sex and Politics,* by Starhawk (Boston: Beacon Press), pages xxvi–xxvii. Copyright 1982, 1988, 1997 by Miriam Simos. Reprinted with permission of Beacon Press, Boston.

To view copyright terms and conditions for Internet materials cited here, log on to the home pages for the referenced Web sites.

During this book's preparation, all citations, facts, figures, names, addresses, telephone numbers, Internet URLs, and other pieces of information cited within were verified for accuracy. The authors and Saint Mary's Press staff have made every attempt to reference current and valid sources, but we cannot guarantee the content of any source, and we are not responsible for any changes that may have occurred since our verification. If you find an error in, or have a question or concern about, any of the information or sources listed within, please contact Saint Mary's Press.